Transformation Timebomb

150 practical business adaptations for the digital age

Gavin Russell

Transformation Timebomb
150 practical business adaptations for the digital age

First paperback edition July 2019

Book design by meadencreative.com

ISBN: 978-1-9161400-0-4 (paperback)

ISBN: 978-1-9161400-1-1 (ebook)

www.gavinrussellconnect.com

Contents

Introduction

1.

The status quo is broken. The political, economic, social, and commercial certainties that have underpinned our way of life are dramatically changing. How people live, work, and play is rapidly transforming, not just in the West but throughout the world. The balance of power is shifting as accepted wisdoms are disrupted by a very different reality.

Innovations in autonomous and electric vehicles, 3D printing, advanced robotics, new synthetic materials, and the Internet of Things are transforming how people interact with their physical world. Genetic breakthroughs are improving our ability to deal with many of the major health challenges of our age. Enhancements in renewable energy and storage look set to break our dependence on fossil fuels.

Geopolitical uncertainty and a rapidly evolving economic environment are challenging the accepted world order. GDP is slowing across the world, while improvements to productivity have been in decline for 20 years. The exhaustion of natural resources, slow economic growth, and steep inequality are forcing governments to completely rethink their economic models.

At the same time, emerging digital infrastructures are reshaping the forces of production and consumption. Increasing fluctuations in underlying costs are disrupting business models and organisational structures. The information revolution is driving new accountabilities. The evolving demand and supply of human capital is changing where, when, how, and why people work.

If that were not enough, these changes are accompanied by a rapid shift in society, as people are losing trust in the establishment and polarising around the individual issues that matter most to them. The expectations on businesses are radically evolving, not only from customers, but from the communities that businesses work in, the workforces they rely on, and the investors that fund their growth.

All of these developments have fundamentally changed the questions that businesses need to answer. Instead of a race to cut costs, pursue ever-greater efficiencies, and deliver short-term financial performance for shareholders, businesses need to find new ways to stay constantly relevant in unpredictable and fast-moving markets, to compete in completely different economic systems, and to effectively engage all of their stakeholders in very different ways.

Unfortunately, many businesses continue to answer yesterday's questions. The established thinking, processes, systems, and infrastructures that have traditionally driven success are so deeply entrenched that they limit an organisation's ability to address the new challenges of the digital age. So much time, effort, and resource has been invested in the past that businesses struggle to let go of their commitment to old courses of action.

The fear of unknown risks, falling tactical rewards, potential failure, or 'rocking the boat' are powerful forces that keep organisations and leaders wedded to the same approaches. The pressures of the day job are often overwhelming, restricting the time and resources available to plan ahead, while existing metrics emphasise failure against old definitions of success. Meaningful, lasting change is often perceived as too difficult, painful, or dangerous to pursue.

In contrast, many other organisations, both start-ups and long-established corporations, are thriving in this new world. They are already adapting to the changing reality and evolving their approaches and strategies to capitalise on exciting new prospects or defend against disruptive new threats.

Some are creating adaptable businesses that innovate better and faster while improving customer loyalty. Others are developing companies that operate at speed, while remaining in dynamic equilibrium with market forces. Many are building more engaged, higher-performing workforces that operate at lower fixed costs and risk.

Recent history suggests that time to adapt is running out. Every month seemingly brings a new example of an organisation – young or old, big or small, business-to-consumer (B2C) or business-to-business (B2B) – that has suffered by not adjusting to the new reality. While Kodak and Blockbuster are often referenced, they are joined by technology giants such as AOL, BlackBerry, Motorola, Netscape, and Nokia. Business titans like Carillion, General Motors, and Xerox. Retail stalwarts like Woolworths, Borders, Toys R Us, RadioShack, and HMV. No industry, no sector, and no business is immune.

The transformation timebomb is ticking.

2.

I first became aware that the status quo was breaking at the start of the 2010s. The global financial crisis of 2008 had dramatically impacted many organisations' appetite for long-term planning and investment. Understandably, many companies were shifting their approach to focus on short-term gains, concentrating on their proven strengths while reducing costs and incrementally improving productivity.

However, despite this focus, returns were becoming harder and harder to achieve. Having consulted at and worked directly for a wide range of companies over the previous 15 years, it was apparent just how many organisations in my network were struggling to remain competitive. Well-funded enterprises with strong propositions run by highly intelligent and capable people were unable to meaningfully improve their results. And the harder leaders and decision-makers worked, the more results plateaued or even fell.

Noticeably, the same issues cropped up time and time again. Established approaches were less competitive. Incremental operational improvements no longer delivered competitive advantage. And it was harder to attract, engage, and extract performance improvements from human capital. I didn't know it then, but the tried-and-tested approaches that had served organisations so well previously were no longer fit for purpose. In fact, some of them were doing more harm than good.

Working as both a business leader and consultant over the past decade, I've been lucky enough to work with some amazing organisations, ranging from technology start-ups to management consultancies to large multinationals. This not only gave me exposure to a variety of contrasting commercial environments, but also allowed me to develop the ideas and concepts explored in this book in a range of real-world settings.

Combining this hands-on experience with business community feedback and empirical evidence from across the world enabled me to develop a range of ideas that can be applied to a number of different businesses and contexts. I wrote this book in the hope that these observations and insights might help organisations and individuals navigate the continued uncertainty that lies ahead.

3.

This book will help you discover the adaptations that deliver competitive advantage in the digital age. It can help organisations untangle themselves from the practices of the past and build dynamic businesses that capitalise on the amazing opportunities that the digital world presents. It offers ideas, insights, and inspiration to help organisations build relevant, sustainable, and competitive businesses. And it provides tangible evidence to encourage leaders to do it before it's too late.

In order to do this, the book addresses three core questions at the heart of the latest industrial revolution. First, what are the major forces reshaping the commercial world? Second, what is the actual impact of those forces on businesses and what questions do they raise? Third, what can businesses do that is both powerful and practical, overcoming the institutional inertia that prevents many from evolving?

To address these questions, the book is divided into two parts. The first part explores nine forces that are fundamentally altering the way the world works. This will help executives and leaders to understand the scale, speed, breadth, depth, and comprehensiveness of the changes shaping the world right now. By understanding these forces, leaders and decision-makers will be equipped to understand and address the causes, not just the symptoms of change, and be better prepared for an increasingly unpredictable future.

The second part of the book establishes the tangible impacts of those forces on the business world and suggests ways to successfully adapt to the new reality. Each chapter revolves around an established strategic management lever (e.g. strategy or operations), and is split into two sections.

The first section examines the new questions that the forces are raising, helping leaders better understand the specific opportunities and threats that will have the greatest influence over their future success. The second half provides pragmatic, scalable, and proven recommendations to deal with the impacts.

We'll explore the importance of planning, purpose, and organisational trust, and the essential role that authentic culture plays in delivering competitive advantage. We'll assess the impact of traditional organisational structures and leadership styles on performance, while considering new ways to liberate teams and reduce organisational drag.

We'll investigate how evolving consumer expectations are redefining the relationships between business and their customers as well as the evolving importance of operational functions. Finally, we'll explore how the changing value of human capital is forcing organisations to rethink how talent is acquired, engaged, and inspired to perform.

4.

The insights provided in this book require a shift in how organisations approach change. While change is undoubtedly hard, the challenges of the digital age cannot be delegated, dealt with using short-term tactical fixes or indefinitely ignored in the hope they'll go away. Successful transformation in the digital age requires a switch in thinking at the heart of most organisations.

For that reason, this book is predominantly written for CEOs and their executive teams. Many of the challenges and recommendations impact entire organisations and therefore require coordinated company-wide responses. While many of the ideas will be delivered by teams across their organisation, their success is wholly reliant on the C-suite taking the initiative, owning the issues, and being fully accountable for the results. It is incumbent on senior leaders to not only endorse change but constantly empower their teams to implement it.

Notwithstanding this focus, the ideas and concepts can be used by any leader striving to improve their function's performance. For example, the insights in *Chapter 7: Positioning for Success, Chapter 8: Operational Excellence,* and *Chapter 9: Leveraging Human Capital* will be just as useful to Talent Acquisition Directors as they are to CEOs. Share the content of this book with anyone in your organisation who you feel may benefit from its observations or recommendations.

Similarly, while the ideas will likely resonate most strongly with mid-sized, private-sector enterprises (roughly between 500 and 5,000 employees), many of the concepts can be applied to much larger or much smaller businesses. Equally, they may be relevant to public-sector organisations struggling with the same challenges or educational institutions looking to provide an alternative perspective for their students.

5.

In many ways, this is a guidebook rather than a textbook. The challenges of the digital age are so varied and change so constantly that an operating manual with specific instructions is too inflexible to be of any use to anyone for very long. And as not all businesses are at the same inflection point, not all leaders want or need to focus on the same challenges.

Instead, this book provides guiding principles to help leaders navigate themselves and their organisations through this time of change. It brings together ideas and recommendations from different parts of the business world into one place and organises them, helping executives make sense of the tidal waves of information and opinion. It suggests tactical frameworks to approach the various challenges that businesses face, enabling organisations to remain focused on key objectives while giving them the flexibility to adapt solutions to their individual situation.

The book has therefore been written in defined sections that leaders can dip in and out of, depending on their need. Each chapter includes a one-page summary framework that leaders can quickly and easily refer to or share with their teams (copies can be downloaded from **www.gavinrussellconnect.com**). While the impacts and recommendations are greater than the sum of their parts (as there is a level of co-dependency between the management levers), each chapter in part 2 can be read in isolation to focus on the areas that matter most to you.

PART 1

The Forces

CHAPTER 1

Political, Economic, and Commercial Instability

The accepted market certainties that most Western businesses have been built on are being radically undermined. Thanks to increased political and economic uncertainty, a corresponding drop in global cooperation, and a rapid decline in trust of the establishment, we are seeing the greatest shift in global political power for over 70 years.

Our current macroeconomic infrastructures are weakening and are increasingly unable to keep pace with demand. A revolutionary new economic system has been created that bypasses the traditional capitalist market approach that has dominated for the past two centuries.

Technology is empowering a fundamental change in consumer behaviour. Having lost trust in established institutions, customers are increasingly engaging directly with peers and suppliers via the internet for information and products. They are connecting to more markets, fuelling their expectations of speed, choice, and innovation. Companies now have to engage users in much more personalised, valuable, and immediate ways. They expect the organisations they buy from and work with to make positive contributions to society, not just to deliver short-term financial performance to shareholders.

In this chapter, we examine these forces in more detail. We explore key political, economic, and market dynamics to understand how they are destabilising the established world order and reshaping commercial realities. By understanding the causes of change and not just the symptoms, leaders at all levels can develop more effective strategies and business models to navigate the uncertainty ahead.

Force 1: Geopolitical uncertainty

The geopolitical unpredictability of the past decade is set to continue for the foreseeable future. Changing politics means companies must grapple with increased costs, supply chains that are under pressure, economies of scale that are harder to achieve and restricted movement of talent, innovation, and capital.

The decline of liberal capitalism

For the past 40 years, modern liberal capitalism has been the defining political economic model across the globe. When communism collapsed in the 1980s, liberal free-market democracy was the only universally appealing model of state-driven economics left standing. For decades, politics was dominated by a centrist agenda, where politicians from both left and right signed up to liberal free markets. Broad free markets and free trade agreements gave the promise of prosperity, which underpinned political and economic stability for decades – providing a level of economic certainty for governments, organisations, and electorates alike.

However, the global financial crisis of 2007/8 questioned the stability of this model. Sticking to the status quo no longer delivered the same results. Free markets and free trade no longer cascaded prosperity through society.

Against this backdrop, globalisation and entrepreneurialism did not seem as unshakeable as they once were. Electorates struggled to support an economic doctrine that meant their jobs could be outsourced and local factories moved to protect the world order. A gap started to appear between politicians, who continued to focus on the positive *net national* effect of globalisation and entrepreneurialism – and electorates who struggled with the resulting *gross local* impact of the same approach. After all, someone who has lost their job and can't pay their mortgage takes little consolation from a 0.2% increase in GDP.

As a result, many Western societies are questioning the constructs of liberal capitalism and the establishment order that has protected and nurtured them for so long, fuelling a backlash against many governments and state institutions. Simply put, people have become disillusioned with the status quo and willing to use the ballot box to force change, even when that change is just as uncertain. Brexit is an obvious example, but so too is the upheaval in the Middle East following the Arab Spring, the rise of the radical right wing in Western Europe, and the election of Donald Trump to the White House.

Falling international cooperation

As a result, the global political status quo has become increasingly fragmented. The rise in nationalist sentiment is leading to a drop in global cooperation. America, which was once the standard-bearer for liberal capitalism and globalisation, is becoming increasingly isolated and is being challenged on a number of geopolitical fronts. The EU no longer backs America on all issues and takes a sharply different view on many topics. China is asserting itself in the Pacific, as Russia is in Eastern Europe and the Middle East.

For example, the US and its allies were on the brink of a full-scale trade war in

May 2018 after Donald Trump's decision to impose a 25% duty on steel and a 10% duty on aluminium from European and Canadian producers.[1] The decision of the US Commerce Department to propose a punitive 220% tax levy in October 2017 on Bombardier jets sold in the US but manufactured in Canada and the UK may result in those countries not buying Boeing products altogether.[2]

In fact, in November 2017, Reuters reported that the world's top 60 economies have racked up more than 7,000 protectionist trade measures since the global financial crisis, with tariffs worth more than $400 billion.[3] National governments are increasingly switching their focus to their own domestic interests at the expense of international cooperation and free trade.

Growing uncertainty

These factors have led to a significant increase in commercial uncertainty. According to the Economic Policy Uncertainty Index (devised by economists from Stanford, the University of Chicago, and Northwestern University), we are in one of the *most uncertain periods* of the past 30 years. The index highlights moments of major economic turmoil, where the election of President Trump was eclipsed only by the 9/11 terrorist attack and the battle over the US fiscal cliff in 2011.[4]

In the UK, a 2018 quarterly survey of 81 financial services firms by the Confederation of British Industry (CBI) and PricewaterhouseCoopers (PwC) found a declining outlook on Britain's overall business climate. Banks and life insurers were especially pessimistic. In fact, optimism in the financial services sector – Britain's biggest source of tax revenue – declined in eight of the previous nine quarters (as of March 2018).[5]

In February 2017, the World Bank announced:

"Weak international trade and subdued investment, among other culprits, conspired to slow world growth to its weakest pace since 2009… Unusually heightened uncertainty about policy direction in major economies casts a long shadow over the prospects of recovery."[6]

Force 2: Rapidly evolving economic landscape

At the same time, the world's existing economic infrastructures are weakening. The over-reliance on unrenewable resources such as fossil fuels is creating significant risk for all organisations that depend on them. In addition, productivity continues to be restricted as the communication, transportation, and energy supply infrastructures that make business life possible become less and less able to keep pace with the speed of change.

Weakening energy foundations

The global economic framework we rely on was built on the communication, power, and transportation infrastructures developed during the first and second industrial revolutions.

Innovations such as the telegraph and the steam engine combined with new railways and coal to drive the first industrial revolution, while telephones and the internal combustion engine combined with oil and roads to power the second.

Although a number of factors made both revolutions possible, *almost all* economic activity within them relied on fossil fuels. Even 200 years later, our economy remains dependent on them for power, light, heat, and transport. From products such as fertilisers and pharmaceuticals to building materials and synthetic goods. From plastics to computers to telephones.

In fact, the International Association of Geophysical Contactors states that fossil fuels account for 96% of the items we use every day.[7] Fossil fuels are fundamental to our economic way of life. This was painfully underlined in July 2008 when the global economic system shut down at the same time as oil reached its highest-ever price. At $147 per barrel, it was too expensive for all of the businesses that relied on it. Some economists, such as Jeremy Rifkin, believe this triggered the financial crash two months later, which brought the world economy to its knees.[8]

However, signs indicate that this fossil fuel-driven economy is reaching the end of its viable life. Although new technologies are enabling the extraction of previously untapped fossil fuel reserves, global supply is being more rapidly exhausted by less developed economies that are growing exponentially.

The inescapable fact is that oil, gas, and coal are finite resources that cannot be renewed. It's only a matter of time before the world runs out of these reserves. End-date projections vary widely, but many analysts give us less than *50 years*. Some, like market research company NRG Expert suggest that known oil deposits will run out in 2052 – and natural gas and coal in 2060.[9] This supply restriction magnifies the disruptions the world is already experiencing.

In the short term, supply is set to be impacted by increasing social and political instability in many fossil fuel-producing states. The political futures of major oil, coal and gas-producing countries such as Kazakhstan, Egypt, Kenya and Uganda are all less predictable than they were ten years ago. Russia is becoming increasingly authoritarian, while the 2018 standoff in the Korean peninsula and the ongoing 'cold war' between Iran and Saudi Arabia means supply is likely to be at increasing risk of dramatic price fluctuations.

If that weren't enough, fossil fuel companies are fighting among themselves to preserve or capture market share. The natural gas industry has positioned itself as a 'cleaner' fossil fuel, at the expense of the coal industry, while OPEC is considering significantly increasing oil production to reduce global prices and undercut the US shale gas industry.[10] As these firms compete harder with each other, the sustainability of supply and the stability of price will be significantly disrupted.

Coupled with this threat to supply is growing popular disengagement with demand. Consumers are increasingly aware of the role of fossil fuels in global warming and pollution and are actively reducing their reliance. Air pollution fears and increasing environmental legislation are seeing demand for diesel cars plummet.[11] A backlash against plastic, a fossil fuel product, is gathering momentum. Awareness of the Great Pacific Garbage Patch (a floating area of rubbish spanning 1.6 million sq km and containing 79,000 tons of plastic) is highlighting the global damage caused by this ubiquitous material.

As a result, consumer behaviour is changing, which is starting to have a major impact on business. Following awareness campaigns around plastic bags and straws, big brands such as Coca-Cola and Evian have committed to 100% recycled packaging. In October 2018, scientists issued a 'final call' to save the world from a climate catastrophe, encouraging global populations to fundamentally change their behaviour. Among other things, consumers are urged to buy less meat, milk, cheese, and butter. To drive electric cars and reduce their reliance on planes. To demand low carbon in every consumer product.[12]

Even governments are proactively pursuing policies to reduce the negative impacts of fossil fuels. Indeed, the Paris Agreement of 2018 gave many nations a common cause for the first time – to combat climate change. Although the US has announced its intention to withdraw, it stands alone. Many other nations have made bold commitments to change. France plans to ban all petrol and diesel cars by the end of 2040, and Norway by 2025. The Netherlands even passed a bill to cut its greenhouse gas emissions level by 95% by 2050. India's government has vowed to phase out all single-use plastics by 2022.[13]

Separately in the UK, the government has pushed the introduction of smart meters to reduce usage, improved the energy efficiency of buildings, and developed incentives to use energy-efficient technology. Citizens in the EU and parts of the US will soon get the 'right to repair'. This 2019 proposal by European environment ministers will force manufacturers to cease building 'end of life' artificially into their products, make them easier to mend, and thereby reduce the demand on many finite natural resources.[14]

Ineffective infrastructures

The weakening of the fossil fuel foundation is just one of the forces reshaping our global economy. Evidence is mounting that the existing state economic infrastructures that evolved during the previous two industrial revolutions can no longer keep pace with current demand. As such, traditional communication, transport, and power frameworks are restricting organisations' efforts to improve productivity.

Most CEOs and senior decision-makers understand that productivity can be improved through better machines, better-performing workers, and better efficiency within their value chain (the process or activities by which a company adds value to an article, including production, marketing, and the provision of after-sales service). While improvements to machines and people can happen in relative isolation, value chain improvements are also reliant on the national economic infrastructures that support them.

For example, a state-of-the-art recycling centre is still reliant on existing transport networks to deliver, collect, and redistribute materials. Genetically modified (GM) food significantly increases crop yields using the same agricultural space, yet it is still reliant on fossil fuels for planting, harvesting, packaging, and distributing to consumers. Fibre optic cables deliver the fastest internet speeds in the world, but many homes and businesses are still connected to this network by copper wires, making those speeds harder to achieve.

An organisation's ability to continually improve productivity is therefore hampered, at least in part, by the inefficiencies of existing national infrastructures. In fact, despite all the fantastic technical innovations coming out of Silicon Valley and other technical centres over the past decade, productivity growth – as measured by GDP – actually peaked in the 1990s and has been in decline ever since in both advanced and emerging economies and across economies spanning both service and manufacturing industries.

Research from McKinsey Global Institute indicated that productivity growth actually fell on average to 0.5% between 2010 and 2014, compared to 2.4% growth a decade earlier.[15] Even though productivity growth fell sharply in the aftermath of the global financial crisis, it had already been falling before the crisis, suggesting a more fundamental issue at the heart of the economic system.

While this productivity paradox continues to baffle many economists and policymakers, the lack of investment in national economic infrastructures cannot be helping the success of the productivity initiatives that many organisations have already invested in. The declining effectiveness of the established infrastructure has precipitated the growth of a new digital one.

New economic models

In the new digital world, economic systems are emerging that bypass the vertically integrated companies and middlemen who dominated the global economy for over half a century. According to economist Jeremy Rifkin, the communications internet is combining with digital transportation and new energy infrastructures to create a brand-new framework that will power future commercial success. [16]

The Internet of Things enables data to be collected on anything and everything as sensors are increasingly embedded in the products we buy and the devices we use. This Big Data shines a light on production in factories, warehouses, fields, and offices. On energy consumption in homes. On the performance of smart vehicles and smart roads. Connected by the communications internet, these digital infrastructures form a distributed network that allows everyone to engage with each other directly – on a global scale and at a very low cost.

This digital infrastructure takes economic power away from traditional organisations. Once the preserve of governments and big businesses, information on everything is now increasingly available to everyone. Organisations can connect directly with consumers or original suppliers. Any business, no matter how big or small, can use enhanced operational transparency to boost efficiency throughout their value chain, improving productivity and reducing costs.

In a digital world, some companies are able to drive their marginal cost (the cost of producing one extra unit after fixed costs have been taken into account) to near zero. For example, the cost of selling one album on iTunes is the same as selling one million. Uber can add another taxi to its inventory without cost by encouraging drivers to join the network using their existing cars. Airbnb does the same for rental properties, rather than acquiring more physical space. As marginal costs get lower and lower, goods and services can be shared directly between producers and consumers without the need for multiple middlemen.

This sharing economy is the first new economic system since capitalism and socialism emerged in the 17th and 19th centuries respectively. Entire industries have been and continue to be disrupted as people share goods and services directly. Launched in 1999, Napster completely changed the music industry. Social media has forever changed how we consume news. Wikipedia serves information to hundreds of millions of users every month, yet all its content is produced for free by external producers, enabling it to destroy the printed encyclopaedia market in a few short years.

New businesses emerge every day with lower operating costs than vertically integrated businesses. Across all industries, the status quo is being disrupted, as the forces behind production and consumption are reshaped.

Force 3: Shifting stakeholder expectations

The huge shifts in geopolitics and macroeconomics, combined with technological innovations, are changing stakeholder behaviours. Across the board, stakeholders from consumers to employees to candidates are losing trust in established organisations. Instead, they are engaging directly with peers and suppliers to get access to information and products. And when they do engage with companies, their expectations are very different to the past.

Growing distrust of the establishment

In fact, the erosion of stakeholder trust and loyalty is impacting organisations in *every market*. A 2017 Trust Barometer published by marketing giant Edelman reported a global crisis in consumer trust. Over half of the 33,000 respondents across 28 markets said they don't trust *any* organisation.[17]

In recent years, trust has been dramatically undermined. From misleading information in the Brexit vote to Volkswagen cheating on emissions tests and Facebook failing to protect its users' data. Not only do these failures damage the organisations responsible – but the *entire industry* they operate in. Facebook's data scandal led to a backlash against Google, Twitter, and Amazon. Billions were wiped off the car manufacturing market following VW's admission.

These days, stakeholders are less willing to accept information that companies broadcast about themselves and their products. And they're less likely to give industries the benefit of the doubt. Reputations are easily damaged. Loyalty is hard to earn – and even harder to retain. And from this, more and more people are turning to social media and the internet to inform their decisions, be it buying products, getting recommendations, or working with organisations. Business are finding it harder and harder to directly influence stakeholders' decisions.

Personalised, valuable, and immediate experiences

As direct influence declines, organisations have to engage their stakeholders in new, more compelling ways. Consumers expect their interactions with a company to be personalised, valuable, and immediate. Just look at Coca-Cola's named bottles and Nutella's personalised labels. Or Amazon and Spotify's recommendation systems, which enable customers to discover new insights based on history, preferences, and peer activity. These personalised experiences are designed to re-establish trust and loyalty in a sceptical world.

In this digital age, consumers can connect to more markets and more suppliers. This in turn fuels their expectations when it comes to speed, choice, and innovation. If they're not satisfied with a company, technology allows them to switch easily and quickly. In 2017, Salesforce polled 7,000 consumer and business buyers and found that 70% believe technology has made it easier for them to take their business elsewhere.[18]

To combat this growing cynicism and decline in trust, businesses are shifting their marketing approaches. Traditional push approaches, such as print advertising, where core messages are broadcast to many, are being replaced by pull methods, such as search engine optimisation (SEO) and search engine marketing (SEM), where companies influence customers more indirectly. Using less intrusive methods that leverage social media and third parties, businesses are establishing loyal followings that draw consumers to their products, strengthen awareness, and increase demand.

With this method, reputation becomes critical. Indeed, relationships between forward-thinking companies and their customers are characterised more as peer-to-peer (P2P) two-way exchanges. Businesses that are succeeding in this new world are those delivering more personalised customer experiences and offering immediately available, relevant content.

The importance of purpose

As society has become more sceptical, an organisation's purpose has become a much more important driver of stakeholder engagement. Purpose is the reason an organisation exists. For example, Google 'organises the world's information and makes it universally accessible and useful' while Accenture's purpose is to 'help clients become high-performing businesses and governments'. A company's purpose defines why it is in business and forms the basis of the emotional contract with all of its stakeholders. Having a purpose provides clarity, aligns leaders and workers, and gives consumers a reason to engage and remain loyal.

To be successful in today's market, organisations must play a role that benefits society – not just their shareholders. It's less acceptable or commercially sensible to focus exclusively on short-term financial performance at the expense of long-term credibility. Consumers stop buying from companies they believe are not contributing back to the world around them. Talented workers stop performing at their best, or even quit working for organisations that don't share a similar sense of purpose to their own. Clients stop partnering with companies that may harm their reputation. And shareholders stop investing in organisations that have declining long-term relevance or potential.

Google's employees have already forced the company to ditch a US military contract as they didn't want to be 'in the business of war'.[19] European consumers are 'tax-shaming' large multinational organisations such as Starbucks, Google, and Amazon, even though those business are not doing anything illegal.[20] Perhaps most significantly, major investors are starting to recognise the financial imperative of purpose on the success on their portfolios. Larry Fink, CEO of BlackRock (an investment firm with $1.7 trillion in active funds), wrote a warning in 2018 to CEOs across the world:

"Society is demanding that companies, both public and private, serve a social purpose. To prosper over time, every company must not only deliver financial performance, but also show how it makes a positive contribution to society. Companies must benefit all of their stakeholders, including shareholders, employees, customers, and the communities in which they operate".[21]

A Sense of Purpose, Larry Fink's annual letter to CEOs, January 2018

There is a growing sense that without a clear sense of authentic purpose, organisations cannot be successful. They too easily succumb to short-term pressures to distribute earnings at the expense of long-term investments that drive growth. They lose customers to competitors who have more clearly defined their purpose and more credibility with consumers. They lack staying power when the going gets tough, as talent is not engaged enough to strive for success.

Summary:

- The geopolitical, macroeconomic, and market certainties that most Western businesses were built on are changing irrevocably.

- Political protectionism and nationalism are driving commercial uncertainty, restricting growth, disrupting global supply chains, and undermining long-established business models.

- The global economy is too reliant on fossil fuels, which are increasingly unpopular and operationally unstable, driving greater uncertainty and volatility for businesses to navigate.

- Incumbent state infrastructures developed during previous industrial revolutions are delivering diminishing returns, limiting productivity improvements despite advances in machines, workforce performance, and efficiency.

- New digital infrastructures are empowering new business models, where near-zero marginal costs are disrupting incumbents in all industries and reshaping the forces of production and consumption.

- Widespread distrust in private and public institutions has led consumers to bypass traditional organisations and connect directly with peers and third parties.

- All stakeholders matter, not just shareholders, and all expect transparency.

- Stakeholder expectations – be they consumers, clients, candidates, employees, suppliers, or investors – have risen dramatically, making it hard to earn trust and even harder to keep it.

- Organisations need to constantly re-establish trust and loyalty through more personalised, valuable, and immediate experiences.

- Organisational purpose is now a much more important driver of stakeholder engagement. To be successful, organisations need to show that they play a role that benefits society and not just their shareholders.

CHAPTER 2

Operational Unpredictability

Throughout history, machines have made people's lives easier and more efficient – on the farm, in the home, in manufacturing, and in the office. From Caxton's printing press to Hargreaves' spinning jenny to the production-line evolution initiated by the likes of Henry Ford, technology has long given people and organisations the ability to do more. But now, technology is not just changing the means of production, but also the very markets that businesses operate within.

In this chapter, we explore the critical forces that are driving these changes and transforming the commercial realities of running a business. We examine the declining dominance of production efficiency and the vertically integrated company, and the increasing effectiveness of partnering with external specialists. We look at the opportunities and risks associated with access to more data, and review the changing demand for talent.

Force 4: Customers and competition are reshaping how companies operate

Evidence is mounting that traditional commercial approaches are not as effective as they once were at delivering competitive advantage. Changing customer expectations, fluctuating operating costs, and growing demand for speed and agility are reshaping operational realities. While this presents challenges, it also offers opportunities for forward-looking businesses to take advantage.

Customers are demanding more than just production efficiency

For decades, the commercial world has been dominated by the doctrine of 'efficient production'. In this, businesses aimed to produce goods and services at the lowest possible cost by continually improving operational and managerial processes. This way, they incrementally increased their outputs while tightly controlling their inputs. Lower costs enabled higher margins for similar goods and services. A broadly predictable and stable economy allowed organisations to take long-term views on competition and risk, leading many businesses to vertically integrate their value chains to maximise efficiency.

However, efficient production is no longer a key driver of competitive advantage. Technology has raised customer expectations to new heights and customers now expect organisations to deliver great products without defects at low cost. What's more, they expect companies to continually improve that offering – sometimes even *after* the point of purchase.

Just look at the continuous app and operating system updates provided by technology companies months and even years after purchase. Once unique to iPhone users, this is now industry-standard. In an increasingly distrustful world, competitive advantage is delivered through improved user experiences, be it better innovation, engaging organisational purpose, improved customer interactions, or all three. Efficient production is no longer a competitive differentiator – it is a minimum expectation.

Having realised this, many businesses are refocusing their efforts around the customer. They are shifting their focus away from generating volume offerings at the lowest cost to higher-value propositions that encourage engagement and loyalty. When applied across every part of the value chain (including outsourced service providers and external partners), the approach is proving to be highly effective.

A great example of this is Delta Airlines. In 2005, the airline's traditional approach led it to file for bankruptcy, forcing it to change their thinking. Delta's new model was based upon 'redefining the flight experience', while simultaneously giving staff a better employment experience. By 2016, the airline had record profits, received credit from inside and outside the industry, and wound up on lists for customer affinity and the best places to work.[1]

After Lenovo purchased IBM's PC business division in 2005, it went through a similar transition. Instead of focusing on a fast, efficient supply chain to deliver volume units to large businesses, Lenovo shifted to giving customers a 'complete experience'. It now regularly involves customers in decisions, and its online fans even influenced the logo design and ensured the firm was producing the right assets. In a highly competitive and shrinking market, Lenovo is outperforming its Windows PC competitors in both sales and market share.[2]

As many value chains reconfigure around experience and not production efficiency, CEOs and senior decision-makers are being pushed towards a consumer-centric approach, rather than a product-centric one. They are reconsidering how their entire value chain, including the parts sourced from external partners, is geared to deliver better experiences for their customers.

Cost fluctuations are reshaping business models

Vertically integrating a business was once considered the best approach to optimising transactional costs. Keeping most work activities inside a business not only enabled organisations to squeeze out incremental improvements in production, but also ensure product quality, reduce supply risk, and deliver commercial advantage by increasing barriers to entry for the competition.

However, the internet changed all that. The impact of marginal costs being reduced to near zero has been accompanied by falling transactional costs, in turn reducing the effectiveness of the vertically integrated business.

It's easier to find external specialists with the latest services and products built to a higher standard than can be achieved internally. As markets have opened up, they've become much more competitive, enabling firms to acquire better products at lower prices than they can produce themselves. As technology enables more efficient collaboration across the supply chain, tasks that once required large bureaucracies now require much less administration, reducing the need for middle managers and multiple layers of hierarchy. Arguably, vertically integrated companies that predominantly leverage internal teams with higher fixed costs are now at a competitive disadvantage.

The sharing economy discussed in *Chapter 1: Political, Economic, and Commercial Instability* is also disrupting many established markets. Sharing enables markets to improve the utilisation of existing assets. Fewer assets are required to service demand, reducing sales, which in turn drives up the amortised costs (the remaining debt left to pay) of any new products entering the market. This fundamentally undermines the financial equilibrium of any businesses with inherently large fixed costs.

For example, Zipcar gives users on-demand access to drive cars by the hour or day in high-demand locations around the world, replacing the need for car ownership. According to AlixPartners, car-sharing services led to 500,000 fewer new car sales by 2014 and will lead to an additional 1.2 million fewer new car sales in America alone by 2021.[3] The promise of autonomous vehicles will build upon this sharing premise, extending market coverage and ease of access and leading to an ongoing reduction in demand for private vehicle ownership.

By 2030, PwC have forecast that the transport sector will require 138 million fewer cars in Europe and the US.[4] As fewer cars are sold, the amortised costs of producing new cars will go up to cover manufacturers' fixed costs. As such, the next decade will be challenging for large business with high fixed employment, real estate, and equipment costs.

The growing effectiveness of external specialists

Changing cost models, consumer demand, and customer-centric approaches are driving a shift in organisational structures from the vertical to the horizontal. In fact, as external markets open up and costs come down, using more outside specialists across more parts of the supply chain becomes an effective response to the challenges of the digital age.

Companies can now deploy higher-quality external specialists for lower costs than their permanent employees. Better outcomes can be achieved with reduced risks and liabilities. Organisations can react faster and more effectively to changing market demand. Specialists can spend more time continuously improving their products and services to remain relevant to increasingly demanding consumers.

In fact, horizontal alignment is empowering many organisations to be much more focused on their core purpose, delivering better customer experiences without the competing distractions associated with vertical alignment.

Take Fever-Tree, a UK drinks mixer company founded in 2005. Building on the success of the small-scale premium gin market, Fever-Tree has grown into a £1.8 billion success thanks to its brand name, reputation, market position, and ability to execute. However, the company provides only the raw materials, contracting out the supply, bottling, and distribution of all its products to specialist suppliers. In just 2.5 years, its stock multiplied 12 times, its profits quintupled, and its investors received earnings of 60 times or more. All with just 40 employees, including directors.[5]

Fever-Tree is not an isolated example. Kylie Cosmetics is run by Kylie Jenner, the youngest member of the Kardashian-Jenner family. Already thought to be worth $900 million as of July 2018, the company has sold more than $630 million of make-up since 2015 when she first launched a $29 'lip-kit'. All of this has been achieved with just 12 employees. Production of the cosmetics and everything else has been outsourced, allowing the business to focus on building followers and loyalty on a range of social media channels.[6]

Force 5: The information revolution is driving new opportunities and accountabilities

In 2017, *The Economist* stated that data and its mining is to this century what oil was to the last.[7] It is the key to driving growth and change. Much like oil, data can be extracted, refined, valued, bought, and sold in many ways. It has become one of the most critical commercial assets for companies to leverage. While there are huge risks if organisations get it wrong, there are great commercial opportunities for those who succeed.

More and better data is commercially critical

According to International Data Corporation, the collective sum of the world's data will grow from 33 zettabytes in 2018 to 175 zettabytes (ZB) by 2025, representing a compounded annual growth rate of 61%.[8] A zettabyte is a trillion gigabytes. To put that into context, storing 175ZB on Blu-ray disks would get you to the moon 23 times (Source: David Reinsel, IDC, ibid).

However, the majority of that data is unstructured, complex, and delivered in real time. Unlike the historical databases most organisations are used to, data today comes from voice, text, video, photos, social media, footfall through commuter turnstiles, sensors in vending machine or on wind turbines. While this causes complexity in how data is captured, the data itself has enormous value, as it gives context and meaning to the customers or events being recorded.

This explosion in scale, speed, and variety of information improves not only the quantity of data available to companies, but also the quality. Automated data capture means that organisations can build a deeper, more detailed understanding of customer preferences and behaviours, and anticipate needs faster and better. This richer data inherently adds more value, and it also creates more opportunities. Organisations that are harnessing this information explosion are dramatically improving their performance. Having more and better data is critical to commercial success.

To leverage the additional value, many companies share information and combine their own data with external datasets to improve overall quality. In the US, the Oncology Precision Network allows physicians across multiple states, hospitals, and clinics to share data for around 50,000 new cases a year. In doing so, they are changing the world of oncology – and dramatically increasing the opportunity to offer effective treatment plans to patients.[9]

Better analysis, better insights, better performance

As well as the explosion in information, there are similar improvements in the field of data analytics. New analytical approaches are enabling better extraction, interpretation, and monetisation of this unstructured data, delivering critical insights that were previously invisible.

Through enhanced analysis of data, entire sectors are being disrupted. Amazon has changed retail forever through its data-driven approach. Each Tesla car uploads roughly a gigabyte a day on a range of factors,[10] which informs the firm's current commercial approach and future autonomous car offerings.

Some organisations have developed predictive analytics to provide insights into future patterns and behaviours. Consider for example, artificial-intelligence (AI) or cognitive services that can spot business trends, prevent diseases or combat crime.[11] IBM's Watson is the best-known example, enabling organisations to predict customer behaviour, improve market segmentation, and forecast specific risks.

Analysis can even lead to new revenue streams for businesses who spot the opportunity. Originally, Google only profiled user data to improve advertising until employees realised that this data could provide a host of other services. Visual recognition, traffic flow, and personality assessments are all now sold to third parties to enhance Google's offering.

Increasing accessibility, increasing accountability

It's not just companies that are placing greater importance on data. Consumers can now access much more independent information on the companies they buy from, collaborate with or work at. This enhanced transparency drives greater accountability and risk for businesses and leaders.

Many of these expectations have been informed by platforms such as Amazon, TripAdvisor, Twitter, Glassdoor, LinkedIn, and Facebook, who have fundamentally changed the way consumers access information. The reach of rating and review systems is reshaping purchasing decisions, especially for younger generations, who are more sceptical of big brands and more trusting of individuals or independent organisations. These digital natives are now holding companies to a higher ethical standard, with far more visibility on indiscretions (real or perceived) and far less forgiveness if organisations don't constantly meet those standards.

These higher standards are especially relevant when it comes to organisations keeping consumer data. Now, consumers are much more aware of the personal information being collected about them and are wary of how this data is used. If they distrust a company, they are ready to move. As such, the act of collecting data creates customer vulnerability and immense risk if things go wrong. Facebook's Cambridge Analytica scandal saw customers actively restricting or rescinding access to their data.[12] Huge data misuse cases have led to legislation changes, such as the General Data Protection Regulation (GDPR) launched in the EU in 2018.

Force 6: Changes in demand for talent are reshaping the modern workforce

Acquiring and deploying people with the right skills is critical to success for any leader. However, technology is now also redefining work, the workforce, and the workplace.

Automation, AI, and data are redefining work

Just as Henry Ford's moving assembly line transformed work a century ago, huge advances in automation, artificial intelligence (AI), and data are redefining work today. Across industries as varied as manufacturing, healthcare, retail, and professional services, technology is fundamentally changing the nature of work.

Most leaders already know that automation can transform many back-office processes. Through automation, tasks such as data entry, invoicing, accounting, and expenses are more efficiently and effectively delivered. And with fewer mistakes, interruptions, and lost data. However, automation delivers advantages beyond just simple administrative transactions. Robotic Process Automation (RPA) lowers the barriers to automation, opening up more functions and processes for improvement. In fact, in 2016, McKinsey Digital suggested that companies could automate 30% of their activities across 60% of all occupations, just using the technology available at the time.[13]

It's not just back-office interactions that are being transformed. AI is already an established force in the workplace. For years, it's helped medical staff to monitor patients in hospital wards or assisted commercial drivers through GPS. Now, the speed and scale of change is increasing. Augmented intelligence such as chatbots and virtual assistants are revolutionising customer support functions. Healthcare providers are using AI to push solutions beyond traditional clinical settings. In the not-so-distant future, self-driving vehicles and delivery robots will be critical parts of the modern workforce.

Improvements in data-driven HR are already improving the way we plan work, recruit, and engage with talent. Organisations have access to a wealth of data that advanced people analytics is turning into commercially valuable insights. From this, companies can better predict the talent they will need and when they'll need it. The latest recruitment software uses tracking technology with enhanced assessment capability and AI to identify better talent faster than traditional methods. Platforms such as Oracle and SAP deliver greater insights into workforce capability, so organisations can better measure performance, optimise workforce activity, and anticipate challenges.

The changing definition of human capital value

As organisations leverage advantages in technology, the role of people in a business is evolving. The human skills that deliver competitive advantage are being redefined – and companies are rethinking the competencies and behaviours needed to be successful and how to acquire them.

As technology absorbs more of the high-volume, low-complexity tasks in a business, the value of the human workforce moves towards the high-value, complex work. This means that creativity, problem-solving, and imagination are increasingly important skills. Value in the human workforce is now less about completing lots of transactional tasks quickly – and more about the ability to analyse dynamic problems, connect the right people and ideas, and deliver high-quality results.

This is leading many organisations to reconsider their skills supply. Some businesses have already adopted radical approaches to meet this new demand and beat their competition. One approach is 'the liquid workforce' (a term attributed to Accenture). Operating in flatter structures, these teams are organised to rapidly adapt based on the environment they're in. Instead of being organised around tasks, multi-functional teams collaborate to deliver a result. Teams are given greater autonomy, move faster, and can implement strategic changes quickly. Indeed, the success of Uber and Airbnb has largely been attributed to their adoption of the liquid workforce.

For this to work, critical skills must be continuously developed and acquired on demand. Companies such as Unilever, Monsanto, and Citibank are partnering with specialist external training providers to build specific curriculums.[14] Workers are funnelled via Massive Open Online Courses (MOOCs) to keep pace with the skills evolution. Liquid teams are then supplemented by external specialists who plug skills gaps that can't be found in-house, while new technology allows these teams to constantly collaborate, no matter where team members are based.

The demand for speed and agility is creating new talent models

The changing demand for skills, speed, and agility in the workforce has led to new talent models emerging. Online marketplaces have sprung up to deliver specialist talent – without the need for capital-intensive investment costs. These digital work-sharing platforms give organisations access to a global pool of specialists. They connect companies directly to rated independent workers, who can collaborate on various short-term assignments. As such, organisations can access more suitable talent at a fraction of the traditional cost.

The range of work-sharing services available today reflects the growing demand for instant talent. TaskRabbit, an online marketplace that connects freelance labour to local demand, provides access to physical services. Platforms such as Upwork, Fiverr and Freelancer offer knowledge services while crowdsourcing sites such as Topcoder source work from large groups. Amazon Mechanical Turk breaks outsourced work into smaller microtasks and there are even cloud labour platforms such as Cloud Factory who create a virtual assembly line, splitting the work into smaller tasks and delivering it through a mix of automation and people.

New workplace models also enable businesses to leverage talent in urban areas, without paying the traditional premiums for office space. Shared workspaces provide flexible space and pricing packages in a community environment. As more people seek work in urban areas, shared workspaces offer a cost-effective way of accessing and engaging talent. Demand for these solutions is growing, with providers such as WeWork already managing 10 million sq ft of office space, despite only being founded in 2010.[15]

At the same time, companies are introducing proven management practices in workflows to reduce complexity and increase performance, agility, and speed. A great example is GE, who launched FastWorks – a program informed by LEAN start-up principles.[16] It has changed the way GE makes decisions and works with customers. The emphasis is on continuous innovation, space to experiment, and validating assumptions and ideas.

Likewise, Spotify has implemented AGILE principles to develop a scaling business model that uses squads, chapters, guilds, and tribes.[17] The aim is to implement "minimal viable bureaucracy" and balance high team autonomy with high organisational alignment. Organisations who are embracing novel businesses approaches are experiencing benefits across their business.

Summary

- Changing customer expectations are challenging the primacy of efficient production.

- Vertically integrated businesses are less effective at optimising transactional costs.

- The sharing economy is increasing the amortised cost of assets over time, while the advent of zero marginal cost is undermining the viability of many existing business models.

- Demand for speed and agility is pushing operating structures towards the horizontal.

- Data and its mining is to this century what oil was to the last one and key to driving growth and change.

- The information revolution and some organisations' ability to capture and analyse data is enabling new insights that are transforming the fortunes of business.

- However, volumes and accessibility of data are also driving much greater levels of corporate transparency, accountability, and risk.

- Technology is forcing business to reconsider the human skills they need to deliver competitive advantage as well as how they organise work, design jobs, structure the workplace, and plan for future growth.

- Access to on-demand talent through online marketplaces enable companies to fill gaps in their existing workforce at lower costs.

CHAPTER 3

Shifting Talent Supply

In the digital age, people, more than capital, represent the critical factor of production and the dominant form of strategic advantage (Klaus Schwab, *The Fourth Industrial Revolution,* Penguin Random House, 2016). However, this critical component within organisations is undergoing an unprecedented transformation. The global workforce is changing in size, composition, and distribution. It is also changing in aspiration and motivation as people look for more meaning and purpose in their work. Who, how, when, and where people work is fundamentally changing.

To understand the impact on leaders and organisations, this chapter considers the key facts and forces that are reshaping talent supply. From changing population demographics and varying motivational characteristics to the rise in independent workers and evolving government policies, we explore how workforces are changing more than at any other time in the past century.

Force 7: Changing workforce characteristics reconfiguring talent supply

The composition of the global workforce is shifting as populations live longer, forcing more and more people to work longer to fund their extended lives. New generations with very different career aspirations now make up a growing proportion of the global workforce, changing the long-established traditional employment dynamic. Technology is reducing organisations' dependence on localised workforces, connecting companies to new sources of supply.

More of us are living longer, multi-staged lives

A demographic change is occurring that few of us are prepared for. Human lives are becoming much longer than they historically were, and are increasingly out of sync with the models of work and life that have dominated for the past 100 years. According to Lynda Gratton and Andrew Scott in their book *The 100 -Year Life* (Bloomsbury, 2016) a child born in the West today now has a more than 50% chance of living to be over 105, while the odds for a child born 100 years ago living to the same age were less than 1%.

Much of this change has stemmed from improvements in medicine and healthcare. In the early 20th century, medicine focused on tackling diseases associated with infant mortality such as typhoid, TB, smallpox, and diphtheria. Many governments around the world invested in public healthcare provision, improved public sanitation, and infection control and promoted campaigns to inoculate children.

These interventions massively improved child life expectancy. Subsequently, the medical profession turned its attention to the illnesses of middle age. The latter half of the 20th century witnessed huge improvements in the diagnosis and treatment of strokes, high blood pressure, high cholesterol, heart disease, and cancer. Thirty years ago, statins weren't even available, yet they are now the most widely prescribed drug in the Western world, improving the lives of millions.

At the same time, governments have focused on public education to improve society's understanding of how lifestyle choices impact health. The perils of alcohol, sugar, and junk food are now well known and accepted. Government strategies in the UK and elsewhere have markedly reduced deaths from road traffic accidents and smoking. Accompanied by improved regulation and public expectation, this has dramatically influenced the fortunes of tobacco and alcohol companies. Even fast-food businesses such as McDonald's now offer 'healthier' options, including a vegan Happy Meal.[1]

Now, medical science is focusing on the illnesses of older age. We have already seen significant advances in the battle against Alzheimer's. The most common orthopaedic intervention is now hip replacement, which was first performed in 1950 and prolongs people's active life. In the next 30 years, medics expect far better diagnosis and treatment of diseases such as Parkinson's, dementia, and diabetes.

All of these changes result in the size of the workforce getting bigger and living longer, but also remaining healthier, active, and more productive for longer. Gratton and Scott surmised that more people will have to work well into their 70s and 80s to finance a longer life. Through necessity, life will become multi-staged, moving away from the traditional three-stage model of education, work, and retirement. Instead people will probably have two or three different careers supported by a more complex life model. What's more, as robotics and AI replace or augment roles that were once considered stable or predictable, individuals will have to continuously learn and retrain to remain employable.

Shifting characteristics

While the workforce has always been made up of multiple generations working alongside each other, its defining characteristics are set by the generation that make up the largest proportion. Each group has its own distinct approach to work, based on that generation's life experiences. Unsurprisingly, the characteristics of the coming workforce are significantly different to those of the past 60 years.

The present global workforce is dominated by two key generations: baby boomers (born from the mid-1940s to mid-1960s), who make up around 30-35%, and Generation X (born mid-1960s to early 1980s), who make up around 25-30%. These generations grew up during one of the most successful and stable periods in all of human history.

Boomers grew up in the time of great prosperity, driven by the early years of liberal capitalism. Unlike their parents who grew up during the Great Depression, they became big consumers. They aspired to own their homes, have two cars in the driveway and buy more food than they could eat. Their consumerism fuelled world economies. Rapid economic growth after the Second World War delivered long-term job security, which in turn enabled the boomers to fund their growing spending habits.

Generation X, often known as the 'latchkey' generation, due to increasing divorce rates and increased female participation in the workforce, are one of the most highly educated generations. They are often characterised by high levels of scepticism, and are more individualistic, resourceful, and self-sufficient. They engage in consumerism just like their parents, especially investing heavily in their children's futures, while simultaneously believing in a greater work/life balance.

Both generations are united in their commitment to liberal capitalism and its economic certainties. Indoctrinated by their baby-boomer parents, Generation X continued to engage in consumerism, which resulted in more and more debt to fund their lifestyles. The long-term permanent employment delivered by liberal capitalism allowed them to take out 30-year mortgages and multiple credit cards as economic certainty and assumptions of job security underwrote their spending decisions.

However, the workforce's centre of gravity is now shifting towards younger generations with very different characteristics, values, and attitudes to work.

Millennials (also known as Generation Y) are those born between the early 1980s and the late 1990s. Studies project that millennials will comprise nearly 35% of the global workforce by about 2020[2] and three-quarters by 2025.[3] Often described as lazy, narcissistic, and prone to job-switching, this generation is also more open-minded, environmentally conscious, and liberal. They entered the workforce during one of the most politically and economically unstable periods since the Second World War.

This group is now being joined by Generation Z, who according to Bloomberg now comprise 32% of the global population and 40% of consumers.[4] Born after the turn of the century, they have never known a non-digital world and have grown up with climate change, the global financial crisis, and increasing political and social unrest. They are much more globally conscious and ethically motivated. Growing up online has made them experts at detecting the faintest whiffs of insincerity, dishonesty, and a lack of authenticity. The first cohorts are just starting to join the global workforce.

For millennials (and now for Gen Z), finding long-term secure employment is much tougher. Globally, wages are stagnating, making it harder to pay off debt, while a growing proportion are working in the transient gig economy. Since the global financial crisis, there has been a big drop in access to credit, leading to reduced consumption of big-ticket items such as houses or cars. As a result, this increasingly large part of the workforce no longer carries the debt that makes permanent employment a priority, making them much less dependent on organisations.

Instead they are motivated by very different factors. They distrust governments but have higher expectations of the companies they buy from and work at. They have embraced the sharing economy and are the least engaged generation in the workforce, changing jobs more often than other generations.[5] They believe that business should consider all stakeholder interests as well as their profits, but their experience with employers leaves them with little sense of loyalty.[6] They are much more concerned about climate change and conflict. And they see the start-up ecosystem and entrepreneurship as critical to their future, making them much less interested in scaling large corporate hierarchies.

Decoupling work and localised human capital

Traditional workforce models were built on the concept that work was done in set locations by local populations recruited to perform specific roles. The efficient, mechanised production that emerged during the previous industrial revolution was dependent on standardising machinery, processes, and human activity. To enable this, the workforce was clustered together in factories (and more recently, in offices), in clear hierarchies and roles, working defined hours to optimise efficient production. The size and capability of the local population became a critical factor in an organisation's success.

However, technology is changing all of that. It has fundamentally broken the link between location and role. Now, work can be delivered from anywhere at any time. Organisations no longer need to gather everyone under the same roof to realise the benefits of collaboration. Connected mobile devices mean that individuals can deliver work at any time of day (or night). Productivity and collaboration software enable remotely located individuals to be just as effective, if not more so than office-bound colleagues. Indeed, a 2014 study found that remote workers were 13.5% more productive than their comparable office colleagues, equating to almost an extra day's work per week.[7]

Organisations are no longer dependent on human capital to supply critical resources. Martin Ford's seminal book *The Rise of the Robots* (Oneworld, 2015) sets out the significantly enhanced role that technology will play in the workplace in the coming years. Smart factories (where large hierarchies are replaced by self-organising products, devices, and machines) can be run far more effectively with much smaller workforces, reducing the reliance on local lower-skilled workforces.

Highly skilled supply is also being automated. For example, around 40% of all legal jobs will be mechanised in the next 20 years[8] while accountants and auditors are among the highest-risk professions for automation.[9] Even surgeons could be replaced, with Lord Darzi (the surgeon who pioneered keyhole surgery) stating that robots can perform better surgery due to increased precision, greater range of movement, and no tremor.[10]

Force 8: Changing aspirations are redefining employment relationships

As the workforce adjusts to changing geopolitics, economics, and technology, a new concept of work is replacing the traditional long-term, stable, nine-to-five permanent role. Individuals are taking greater ownership of their careers to gain increased access to more meaningful, satisfying, and profitable work. In so doing, they are avoiding the convoluted hierarchies and 'leader-lotteries' that can make or break their career.

While many in the lower-skilled workforce will be subject to more insecurity and will struggle to build any stability, many others in the higher-skilled workforce will be able to spend more time doing what they love for more money and/or greater satisfaction. This is fundamentally changing the employer/worker relationship.

Shifting balance of power

Traditionally, when an employee joined a business, they gave a degree of control in their career development to their employer in return for a level of financial security. While candidates 'owned' their career paths, the job security and career development provided were dependent on employees aligning their career path to the company's objectives.

To be successful, workers had to conform to defined behaviours and values, and were instructed on how to 'fix themselves' at every performance review to fit in. The promise of job security and career development was often used as a critical lever for organisations to control their debt-laden workforce.

However, technology has transformed individuals' ability to control their careers. Workers now have greater access to far more employers around the world, as they can undertake work regardless of location. They have access to multiple specialist online communities to develop relevant skills quickly and cost-effectively, and an always-on network to target better career opportunities. Unencumbered by the same levels of personal debt, they are less dependent on organisations for financial security and more able to make bold career decisions.

Now, instead of fitting their career to the company, they can fit the company to their career. Individuals increasingly select the organisations they want to work for, while businesses move towards hiring people who naturally match their needs. This shift not only allows workers to specialise and spend more time doing what they love, but it also means that organisations have less leverage to control their workforce.

Increased satisfaction and reward

It's not just workers' level of control and choice that is affected, it is also their satisfaction and income. In a study of the independent worker marketplace in 2016, McKinsey Global Institute analysed data from 8,000 respondents from seven world economies including the US and the UK. They found that independent workers had higher satisfaction levels than those in traditional jobs in 12 of the 14 dimensions and were equally satisfied on the remaining two.[11]

The study suggested that free agents are more engaged in their work, relish the chance to be their own boss, and have more control over their working hours. Interestingly, they are happier with their level of income and just as satisfied as traditional workers on their income security and benefits. A 2017 study on the US market by the Freelancers Union and Upwork found that more and more people are going independent by choice, and that freelancing offers greater career stability and helps human capital be better prepared for the future.[12]

A 2017 study of 5,000 workers in the UK, US, Australia, and New Zealand also backed this up, concluding that self-employed people are happier and more engaged with their jobs than any other profession.[13] They found that self-employed people were not only more successful, but also more satisfied with their professional contributions.

The increase in satisfaction is also accompanied by increased income. A 2017 UK study by Intuit QuickBooks found that self-employed people make £33,000 in average annual revenues. That's £5,000 more than the UK average salary, despite freelancers working an average ten hours less per week.[14] In 2017, the average US income for independent workers was $63,500, nearly $10,000 higher than the average for permanent employees.[15]

Reduced effectiveness of traditional management approaches

At the same time, there has been a parallel decline in the effectiveness of traditional management approaches. Workers are increasingly looking for and have access to more meaningful work. They have more control and choice and are less dependent on organisations. However, the management approaches that many organisations continue to use don't seem to have evolved in a century to match these changed realities.

These traditional approaches have their roots in the 19th century. As the second industrial revolution gathered momentum and people moved from rural areas into cities, organisations looked for ways to extract maximum value from their human capital. Two models emerged that are still in use today. Frederick Taylor's 'Scientific Management' initially reduced the number of steps needed to do work and evolved to a full-scale management theory that synthesised workflows to drive economic efficiency and labour productivity.

Taylorism replaced rule-of-thumb work methods with those based on a scientific study of tasks. Each employee was selected, trained, and developed rather than being left to train themselves. Each worker received "detailed instruction and supervision" to optimise the performance of their specific tasks. Work was divided equally between managers and workers, where managers applied scientific management principles and workers actually performed the tasks.

The second model was about leadership. To manage the increased complexity of Taylorism, organisations adopted 'command and control' where instruction came from the top down, giving senior decision-makers complete jurisdiction. This had clear advantages, providing clarity by removing ambiguity in who makes decisions and who follows them. This meant that large groups could be directed quickly with minimal disruption.

At the time, this approach was ideally suited to industrialists. Work became regimented and disciplined. Processes were deconstructed into manageable, measurable tasks, all of which needed to be supervised through multiple layers of hierarchy. Command and control let the new leaders of industry tightly control production, costs, and people.

Today, many leaders continue to follow these same principles. Work is still regimented, disciplined, and controlled. Workers still receive detailed tasks, instruction, and supervision. Teams are still grouped in functional blocks within multi-layer hierarchies.

However, as workers seek increased career control, choice, and job satisfaction, these methods don't work as well. Individuals are less likely to relinquish autonomy over their careers. They don't want detailed instruction and supervision by a manager who probably knows less than they do about their specialism. They won't tolerate convoluted hierarchies, poor leadership, or slow career progression, things commonly associated with traditional businesses. Taylorism and command and control are less and less effective at harnessing today's workforce to deliver productivity and profitability.

Force 9: Increasingly independent, increasingly important

The world is witnessing the rebirth of the independent workforce. As it increases in size, new work-sharing platforms are significantly increasing accessibility, and connecting more people with more opportunities. The independent workforce is now playing a much more significant role in enabling organisations to respond to the speed and unpredictability of demand. At the same time, the barriers to a viable independent workforce are diminishing. The independent workforce is becoming a vital cog in the commercial machine.

The workforce is increasingly independent

The independent workforce is not a new phenomenon. Before the first industrial revolution, much of the global workforce was independent. However, the rise of mechanisation and factories meant that labour was organised in more structured employer-employee relationships as a way to organise and control activity.

While these structured employment relationships have come to dominate the world of work, independent work continued to exist. This is particularly the case in vocations where agility and flexibility are economically sensible such as acting, writing, or construction. However, the independent workforce is now growing faster than any other time in the past two centuries.

In fact, it's much larger than previously predicted. The McKinsey Global Institute report referenced earlier[16] suggests that around 20-30% of the working age population in the US and EU were involved in some form of independent work in 2016. This included an estimated 54 million to 68 million independent earners in the US and 60 million to 94 million in the EU.

Predictions suggest that this figure will grow. *Forbes* magazine stated that if this trend continues at the same rate, 50% of the workforce will be independent by 2027.[17] This growing force, also known as the 'Human Cloud', is already disrupting the way work happens, in the same way that high-speed on-demand cloud computing disrupted IT services.

The relatively recent arrival of digital work-sharing platforms has also dramatically improved accessibility to independent work. Today these platforms (e.g. Upwork, Freelancer, and Fiverr) are used by 15% of independent workers, but the rapid growth of the largest platforms suggests the beginning of significant change. While many of these platforms are still very much in their infancy, they have the power to fundamentally change the relationship between organisations and individuals, similar to how Amazon transformed the retail industry by directly connecting buyers and sellers online.

Increased value of independent workers

The increasing speed, complexity, and unpredictability of demand increases the independent workforce's value to companies. It is already much harder to predict what the key roles will be in the near future and for organisations to define fixed workforce strategies that manage their hiring risks.

New roles and industries are being created faster than at any other time in history. Ten years ago, few would have predicted that Machine Learning and Big Data experts would be some of the most sought-after skill-sets in the world or that electric and autonomous vehicles would be the future of car manufacturing. New and as yet unimagined jobs and industries will grow, sparking demand for skills and experience that cannot be specifically predicted, let alone trained or pipelined for.

Independent workers are better positioned to respond to this uncertainty. Their independence enables them to closely align to their specialism and adapt quickly to changes within markets. Their connection to online networks also makes them the first to know which skills are in demand and learn those skills rapidly. Free from extensive notice periods, they can also be deployed quicker than permanent candidates.

In addition, independent workers are not part of an organisation's fixed cost base. As such, they represent a cost-effective, adaptable resource, enabling businesses to expand their workforce at times of high demand and reduce it when demand drops. With greater levels of specialisation, companies can find people with exactly the right skills to deliver specific results, increasing organisational productivity.

It's hard to imagine large permanent headcounts and traditional learning and development approaches rising to the challenge in quite the same way.

Legacy restrictions for independent workers are diminishing

Traditionally, hiring independent workers has been challenging. Existing government policy frameworks deliberately made it harder to hire independent workers. Policies were geared to a more industrial time when employers were less publicly and privately accountable and when public health and pension safety-net programmes were funded by higher tax receipts received through higher permanent employment.

But in our rapidly evolving world, governments have started to realise that there are significant advantages to building the right conditions for an independent workforce to thrive. It increases labour force participation and increases opportunities for the unemployed to return to work. It increases capital productivity, as underutilised assets and spare capacity are used more effectively. And it stimulates consumption as more people have more capital and more access to products.

Because of this, governments are realising that their guidance can no longer restrict independent work, as it doesn't fit the current status quo. Rather, they must adapt policy and guidance on health, pension, and tax so that independent work can take place, while also safeguarding those in it.

In 2017, the government-commissioned Taylor Review laid out seven principles to address the challenges facing the UK labour market.[18] It advocated a clearer definition of the different employment types, that contract rates exceed the minimum wage, that tax is better aligned with employment, that workers are consulted more, and that holiday and sick pay is enforced (among other things).

Similarly, in the US, a new bill called the Harmonization of Coverage Act was tabled in March 2018.[19] It aimed to simplify employment and create a level playing field. Likewise, the European Commission is reworking the EU's economic policies to extend social protection and other forms of security to all workers, not just employees.

At the same time, the public safety net programmes that once dominated our economy are being replaced by private ones. Independent innovators are stepping into the health and pensions market to offer new products, services, and solutions to help independent workers traverse the gaps in protection left by the decline in permanent roles. Common job benefits – such as health insurance and pension plans – can be set up to travel with a worker as they move from one job to the next. In many cases, these benefits would be paid for by the worker, which makes them attractive to employers, while the flexibility gives independent workers security that was limited in the past.

Talent no longer needs to choose between the satisfaction and fulfilment of independent work or long-term health and pension security of permanent employment. Increasingly, they can have both.

Summary

- The changing characteristics of the global workforce are reconfiguring supply, while shifting aspirations are transforming the motivations of the workforce.

- Technology is not only allowing more parts of an organisation's workflow to be automated, reducing the need for large headcounts, but also to become virtualised, opening access to much bigger and more specialised talent pools.

- More and more workers are taking back control of their careers and gaining access to more meaningful, satisfying and profitable work, allowing them to fit a company to their career, not their career to a company.

- Some existing approaches to management are less effective, as workforces become less loyal and seek greater autonomy and independence.

- The independent workforce is already big and set to get bigger, and it is starting to disrupt the way work is delivered.

- Independent workers are better positioned to deal with the speed, complexity, and unpredictability of the digital world, while many of the legacy barriers to their engagement are falling.

PART 2

Impacts and Recommendations

Introduction to Part 2

The second half of the book establishes the impact of the forces outlined in the first half on the management of organisations, then makes recommendations to address those impacts.

Part 2 is split into six chapters, each focusing on an established management lever that organisations use to engineer success. These include The Plan (which includes strategy), culture, structure and leadership, market positioning, operations, and HR. Each lever is important in its own right, but The Plan and culture are explored first, as they underpin many of the points in later chapters.

As there are many different (and occasionally contrasting) definitions of each management lever, each chapter starts with a clarification of the terms used and a reminder of its relevance in the effective leadership of a business.

To illustrate the consequences and ramifications of the impacts, they are broken down using real-world commercial examples. The impacts are explored in detail, as a thorough understanding of the new questions that leaders are being asked can be just as helpful as specific advice, enabling decision-makers to develop solutions that better fit their individual needs.

The second half of each chapter provides recommendations to address the impacts. Every business is different, so these recommendations are not intended to be a laundry list of sequential steps that every organisation must take. Rather, they are a mix of ideas, concepts, and proven examples to provoke thought and inspire action. They combine broad principles and specific approaches to give organisations the flexibility to pursue and evolve the ideas that resonate most strongly, leverage established methods to deliver quick results, or a bit of both.

Given the complexity of the forces at play, individual recommendations are not tied to individual impacts – some may address several challenges while others address just one. Additionally, there are inevitable overlaps between the chapters as they consider the effects of the same forces. This means that the same impacts will reappear in some chapters. While every effort has been made to minimise any repetition, this is a deliberate approach to ensure each chapter addresses the specific challenges facing that particular management lever. Limitations of space and time prevent an exhaustive list of suggestions applicable to every business, but it is hoped that the guidance is relevant or enlightening to most organisations and situations.

Each chapter concludes with a one-page summary. These are simple tactical frameworks for you to use, either as a handy reference guide or to inform and evolve your ongoing approaches. Free copies can be downloaded at **www.gavinrussellconnect.com**.

As different issues will matter to different companies, there is no perfect sequence to apply the recommendations. However, leaders can use the summary frameworks to structure their approach, starting in the top-left recommendations column and activating the suggestions as they work their way across and down towards the bottom right.

CHAPTER 4

The Plan

A plan is a detailed proposal of how to do or achieve something specific. A plan identifies opportunities and develops tactics to outperform the market. It identifies future risks and natural weaknesses and proactively mitigates their impact. It enables businesses to define achievable goals that the entire organisation can align to, measure progress against those goals, and take corrective action as and when necessary. A plan improves decision-making, enabling organisations to prioritise the right actions and reduce the risk of being overwhelmed by distractions. A plan enables collective ownership so human capital knows where they are going and what's expected of them.

There are different definitions of the core components that make an effective Plan, so for clarity these terms are defined as:

- **Purpose:** This tells everyone – both inside and outside the organisation – why a company does what it does, for whom, and how. Sometimes called The Mission, it explains what the company intends to accomplish by developing and offering products/services and what difference it makes to its customers.

- **Vision:** This tells everyone where the company is going and what it will become in the future, setting the overall long-term direction. It is often bold, inspirational, and a unifying focal point for everyone in the business – guiding both strategic and tactical decisions.

- **Values/beliefs:** This is what the company believes in and stands for. These values or beliefs are constant, intrinsic principles that also guide the conduct and activities of the business, broadly outlining which behaviours are acceptable and which are not.

- **Strategy:** This defines the steps, activities, and methods to overcome challenges on the way to achieving the vision. It is a living, dynamic approach that drives actions and behaviours, and it:

  o Describes the current position and capabilities, builds on strengths, mitigates weaknesses, capitalises on opportunities, and recognises threats.

  o Can be broken down into digestible objectives and goals. Long-term objectives clearly connect the mission (what you do today) to the vision (what you'll do tomorrow). Goals operationalise the direction while sustaining competitive advantage.

o Cascades throughout the organisation so that each function can extrapolate their specific priorities and tactics while remaining aligned with the overall approach.

o Has clear metrics, checkpoints, and financial parameters to accurately measure performance on an ongoing basis and course-correct as necessary.

The whole is often greater than the sum of its parts, and commercial success depends on the effective interaction and alignment of all of the elements in The Plan, constantly adjusting and adapting to changing market conditions.

Why should leaders care?

The Plan is essential for businesses to focus on the right actions. It optimises the use of assets and limited resources to achieve specific objectives. It unifies human capital around a common purpose, helping teams pull in the same direction while striving for improved performance. It creates agility and endurance, enabling organisations to evolve in times of change. Organisations are more successful when they invest their time and efforts in The Plan.

If having a plan is essential, not having one can be catastrophic. Opportunities are missed, money is misused, and risks are magnified. Workforce performance falls and pressure increases as businesses need to speed up just to stand still. Poor or badly executed plans are just as bad, distracting businesses from achieving intended objectives, misusing limited budgets and misaligning resources.

Impact of the forces

The forces of the digital age are fundamentally disrupting The Plan. Demand for greater strategic agility is increasing, while the commercial certainties that plans have relied on are decreasing. Plans have to assimilate a much wider set of considerations as customers, clients, workforces, and shareholders collectively demand very different outcomes. Even with a plan in place, fluctuating markets, increased organisational friction, and falling trust make it harder for leaders to deliver everything within The Plan.

Impact 1: Demand for faster, fresher, and more adaptable strategies

Product and service lifecycles are shortening

In today's markets, companies need to get competitive products and services to their customers quicker than ever. Consumers want more innovative features more regularly. The new economic models discussed in previous chapters are enabling competitors to bring products and services to market sooner. Businesses that are slow to launch new products risk tarnishing their brand or being superseded by competitors. Being a 'fast follower' is no longer an option.

The car industry offers a good example of this. According to CAP Automotive, the gap between replacement model introductions shrank from ten years in the 1970s to about three or four years in 2013.[1] There are significant technical leaps in each model release, with each set of innovations becoming the *expectation* rather than a differentiator. This in turn leads to faster product depreciation, as previous models become less desirable quicker. Alongside growing consumer expectations of lower emissions and rapidly evolving regulations, the pressure on slow-lifecycle car manufacturers is increasing.

The maturity phase of the product lifecycle is also compressing. Long-term product 'cash cows' are becoming a thing of the past, and following market leaders no longer guarantees market relevance. Companies cannot rely on established products and services to provide the bulk of their revenue and must launch new offerings early in the market growth curve.

Samsung lost 66% of the global smartwatch market within a quarter of Apple releasing its first watch,[2] while Nokia couldn't keep up with innovations from Research In Motion, the makers of BlackBerry, who in turn weren't able to keep up with iPhone innovations.

At the same time, external specialists can now deliver instant capability, accelerating the development and delivery of higher-quality offerings. For example, outside partners deliver GPS systems or airbag solutions for cars better than manufacturers can make themselves. In video game production, core platform providers enable developers to bring games to market quicker by removing the requirement for ground-up development. Website costs are slashed – even those with the latest functionality – using ecosystems such as WordPress or Wix. Amazon Web Services (AWS) allows organisations to access huge global processing power without the time delay or cost of building such capabilities themselves.

Changing commercial certainties

The commercial certainties that many strategies were built on are being undermined. Plans must factor in disruptions to existing supply chains, new sources of competition, and changing access to resources and technology. As a result, many organisations are considering completely new approaches just to continue delivering existing products and services – let alone launch new ones.

For example, Just-In-Time (JIT) supply chains operating across national borders are at increasing risk. Changing politics and economics are creating friction for components ordered from internationally distributed contractors that need to arrive at a precise time and place for assembly.

> The crankshaft used in BMW's Mini crosses the English Channel three times in a 2,000-mile journey before it rolls off its UK production line. Any increased border friction will have a disproportional knock-on effect across BMW's supply chain, forcing it to find new ways to manage risk.[3]

What's more, the cost of doing business is rising as global trade wars increase transactional costs, limit growth opportunities, and decrease market access to producers.

> The mounting trade rift between China, Europe, and the US is already impacting Jaguar Land Rover, who announced 4,500 job cuts (January 2019) as Chinese consumers delayed their vehicle purchases due to changes in import duties.[4] Toymaker Hasbro is moving more of its production out of China to avoid import duties, and Harley-Davidson is shifting production away from the US to avoid the EU's retaliatory tariffs.[5]

Finally, the unpredictability of fossil fuel supply and its associated price volatility severely impacts dependent organisations operating on fine margins. This not only includes transportation and energy companies, but also businesses that use oil derivatives (such as plastics) or in pharmaceutical production, building materials, or synthetic goods. This is forcing many companies to shift their exposure to alternative supply options.

Numerous cities are reducing their fossil fuel usage to mitigate the risk of supply.

> Cape Town aims to source 10% of its electricity from renewable energy by 2020 and reduce greenhouse emissions by 1 million metric tons.[6]

Unpredictability combined with an increasingly negative public perception is also causing organisations to distance themselves from fossil fuels.

Apple, Goldman Sachs, Pearson, P&G, Walmart, and Wells Fargo have joined 150 companies in the RE100 commitment to use 100% of their power from renewable energy.[7]

Traditional plans are less competitive

These days, many tried-and-tested plans are less competitive. Value chains are distorting, leading to reductions in fixed and variable costs, highlighting the weaknesses of older, inflexible business models. The information revolution and increasing consumer scepticism are driving greater transparency and accountability in organisations, exposing aggressive, socially questionable, margin-hungry approaches.

For example, the digital economy is reducing the need for intermediaries. Organisations can now reach consumers and clients directly via e-commerce platforms without multiple middlemen, and this enables them to sell similar or identical products at lower costs. Direct-to-Consumer (D2C) solutions aren't reliant on physical real estate for exposure and can use the data revolution to transform customer experiences.

Airbnb upended the holiday and experience market, Casper is taking on the mattress industry, and businesses like Soylent are building entirely new product categories.[8] Established brands are fighting back against these newcomers, with Nike launching 'Consumer Direct Offense' – a faster pipeline to directly serve customers at scale[9], while Gillette launched 'Gillette Club' to take on Harry's and Dollar Shave Club.[10]

In this climate, businesses that maximise margins above industry standards are in ever-greater jeopardy. Consumer access to information, third-party influencers, and ratings mechanisms create a more transparent and informed arena, enabling buyers to avoid organisations with unjustified margins. Heightened regulation enables them to seek significant compensation when unjustifiable costs come to light.

In September 2018, three of Britain's biggest mobile phone networks (EE, Three, and Vodafone) were caught charging customers for handsets even though they had already paid off the cost.[11] In 2014, State Street Corporation's custody bank was fined $38 million for deliberately overcharging six of its clients a total of $20.2 million, by deliberately adding substantial mark-ups on agreed fees.[12]

Finally, new approaches to analytics have transformed the value of business data, undermining the traditional approach to proprietary data management. Insurance firms are embracing analytics systems to target more profitable sectors, speeding up payments and reducing fraud. The securities industry is using automated algorithms to outperform traditional money markets.

In 2018, BlackRock sacked seven fund managers and shifted billions of dollars to a computer-powered 'quantitative' investment unit. Bristol-Myers Squibb reduced the time needed to run clinical trial simulations by 98% by extending its internally hosted grid environment onto AWS Cloud.[13] Pratt & Whitney is reducing unplanned aircraft engine maintenance using data from next-generation engines to enable proactive maintenance. (ibid)

Impact summary: Dynamic strategies

New offerings are coming to market much faster, while established products are relevant for a much shorter amount of time. The effectiveness of tried-and-tested strategies is declining as operational certainties wane, forcing organisations to continually update their approach. Organisations are being forced to rethink what they do and how they do it just to remain competitive.

Impact 2: Plans must deliver wider and more challenging outcomes

Different success criteria

In today's society, consumers are much more focused on an organisation's purpose, values, and ethics. They measure companies by the role they play in society and their approach to long-term value creation. Their buying behaviour is influenced more by a brand's purpose and less by features and price.

Consumers want to buy from organisations that reflect their values and provide an emotional connection – companies which stand for something more than just shareholder profit. Once seen as a competitive differentiator, customer service is now a bare minimum requirement. Consumers actively avoid organisations that lack authenticity, even if those companies offer lower prices. Plans must now go beyond the utilitarian logic of cost and service to address more subjective and emotive expectations.

For example, sales exploded and stock closed at an all-time high when Nike used Colin Kaepernick for its 'Just Do It' campaign (September 2018) to communicate its social purpose.[14]

Knowing this, shareholders and investors are motivated by increased customer relevance and longer-term sustainability. In addition to Larry Fink's letter mentioned in *Chapter 1: Political, Economic, and Commercial Instability*, Baupost Group CEO and hedge fund billionaire Seth Klarman has called for an avoidance of 'toxic short-termism'. He argues that "shareholder primacy" needs to be replaced with a more balanced approach that reflects the views of other stakeholders, such as employees and the community, for the sake of long-term growth.[15] Numerous investment banks are setting up new funds to tap into this new sentiment.

Swiss bank UBS launched a new global impact equity fund in 2017 that focuses on "long-term growth opportunities which aim to generate a positive social and environmental impact alongside a consistent financial return".[16]

The workforce is also placing much greater importance on alignment with the organisation's purpose. Financial security on its own is less powerful at motivating talent and is being replaced by the desire for more fulfilling and meaningful work, career autonomy, and opportunities to learn. This applies as much to independent workers (self-employed individual freelancers or contractors) as to permanent employees, and to a lesser extent outsourced third parties. We explore these themes in more detail in *Chapter 5: Culture* and *Chapter 9: Leveraging Human Capital*.

Customer experience and innovation are key strategic drivers

Strategies now have to enable personalised, valuable, and immediate experiences at all stages of the customer journey – not just at the point of purchase. Innovation that delivers continuously relevant products and services has become a strategic imperative. Customer demand has to be fulfilled at places of their convenience, particularly online, on mobile devices, and at times that suit them – not in a shop with fixed opening times that they have to travel to.

Instead of delivering fixed products and services and persuading customers and clients to buy them, plans now need to deliver fluid, customisable offerings that can be tailored to meet faster-changing consumer demands. They have to underwrite innovation – constantly listening to audience feedback and encouraging distributed workforces to iterate improvements throughout product and service lifespans. The exploding popularity of customer-centric rather than product-centric plans underlines both the shift in thinking and the success of these approaches.[17]

Now, *all* customer experiences matter. Plans have to improve the entire customer journey, including all of the elements leading up to the purchase – and critically, all the moments after. Many organisations are developing easier, friendlier, and simpler customer journeys to improve relationships and loyalty.

> Insurance company Lemonade is making the underwriting and claims process easier by simplifying the experience, open sourcing their code to allow others to improve it, and ensuring that customer journeys are mobile-friendly.[18] They also donate unclaimed insurance money to a charity of the customer's choice, reinforcing their social purpose.[19]

This theme is explored in greater depth in *Chapter 7: Positioning for Success.*

As customers become increasingly time-poor, have lower attention spans, and have more choices, plans must ensure that products and services are easier to find and more convenient to consume. Strategies have to give consumers more control of their buying interactions, with customised experiences that are configured to work around the buyer's requirements, not the seller's infrastructure.

> To optimise their consumers' clothes-shopping experience, Amazon launched Prime Wardrobe, a try-before-you-buy service where customers can receive up to eight items to try for free for seven days, and are charged only for the products they keep.[20]

Staying ahead of the curve is essential for long-term relevance

As product and service lifecycles shrink, organisations have to accurately and constantly predict demand to ensure that their offerings remain relevant and attractive. More than just inventory management and transactional demand planning, strategies are now leveraging the wealth of customer and market data to stay one step ahead of their competitors.

> Spanish clothing retailer Zara continually forecasts demand, delivering clothes to the high street within two weeks of designs first appearing on catwalks (in contrast to competitors' six months), ensuring their products are both popular and desirable.[21]

Increasingly, this means that organisations have to predict what customers will want before customers even know it themselves! They have to anticipate future demands and problems to develop compelling offerings in time.

> Apple entered the mobile phone market well before mobile phones became the essential device they are today, while Indian conglomerate Godrej & Boyce developed its hugely successful ChotuKool refrigerator for the 85% of the Indian population who *didn't* buy refrigerators.[22]

Constant innovation is increasingly required to improve products, delivery, and experiences – replacing production efficiency as the core driver of profitability and revenue. Customers expect more choice, change their minds more frequently, and are more vocal when offerings don't meet their expectations.

> To break into the smartphone market already dominated by Apple and Samsung, Huawei invested more than $45 billion in R&D between 2008 and 2018, developing new standards in mobile photography and AI.[23]

Impact summary: Deliver more

Plans now have to assimilate different and constantly evolving expectations from customers, clients, distributed human capital, and shareholders. They must move well beyond the traditional safety of operational efficiency to continually deliver improved customer experiences and greater innovation. They must also forecast faster and more accurately to get ahead of the demand curve and remain relevant to increasingly fickle audiences.

Impact 3: Delivering The Plan is harder

More complexity and distractions

With markets moving much faster and in less predictable ways, there are more threats to counter, opportunities to exploit, weaknesses to mitigate, and strengths to build upon.

As a result, businesses find themselves navigating more distractions and disruptions. The amount of information available is increasing dramatically, making it harder for leaders to differentiate between meaningful signals and meaningless noise. The growing volume, variety, and velocity of variables increase the chance of misalignment between actions and goals. All of this makes it harder for leaders to accurately decipher client requirements and remain focused on results instead of tasks. It also makes it harder for workers to make the right decisions in real time.

Moreover, it's harder to forecast market conditions. Plans must allow for unforeseen technological advances, more agile competitors, and unpredictable economics. For example, travel agents didn't anticipate the success of Expedia, taxi firms didn't predict Uber and Lyft, and hotels didn't foresee Airbnb.

Jaguar Land Rover couldn't predict Chinese consumer demand falling 46% in the last quarter of 2018[24], nor could Tesla forecast a drop of 70% in its October 2018 year-on-year sales.[25]

As such, staying strategically aligned is much more complicated than it used to be. Strategies can't be over-prescriptive, because too much detail will make it too rigid and inflexible to respond to market changes in real time. On the other hand, being under-prescriptive leads to a lack of clarity and causes organisational confusion. To deliver, leaders have to continuously flex The Plan in response to market changes, disruptions to supply chains, constantly evolving competitors and changing talent demand.

Increased organisational friction

These increased complexities and distractions magnify the risks of employees diverting from The Plan. The expanded commercial requirements outlined in Impact 2 create misunderstandings and misinterpretations of the strategy, which can lead different parts of the business to pursue conflicting goals.

For example, a strategic objective of improving customer profitability can be interpreted by one part of the business as a directive to increase sales while elsewhere it can be taken to mean a greater focus on customer loyalty (*Chapter 6: Structure and Leadership* explores the phenomenon of 'unintentionality' and the creation of ghost strategies in more detail). Occasionally, this brings different parts of the organisation into conflict with one another, creating friction at key hand-offs in the value chain, damaging organisational culture while negatively impacting customer experience and innovation.

Pressured by accelerating demand, teams prioritise urgent over important, mistakenly concentrating on low-value activities while ignoring higher-value ones. Many managers focus their teams on transactional tasks that are easier to achieve, more straightforward, and have immediate payoffs, giving them the false sense of security that 'doing' will protect them from scrutiny. As time and resources are diverted to low-value activities, opportunities are missed and threats are left undefended.

In addition, growing commercial uncertainty leads many employees to develop a perception of job insecurity, which leads to fear, exacerbating existing negative behaviours and creating organisational friction. The fear of 'rocking the boat' and receiving negative attention often stops workers and managers from constructively feeding back, highlighting problems, or reporting failures, even when it's clear that the intended strategy is being diverted.

The potential lack of clarity around The Plan, organisational purpose, and definitions of success also leads some workers and managers to prioritise their personal agendas over strategic ones. An obvious example is pushing short-term sales cycles to maximise individual commission bonuses at the expense of longer-term company goals.

Shifting realities for leaders

In this business climate, traditional strategic models are proving less effective. Many strategies are based on an assessment of the current situation and assume an understandable, stable, and predictable environment. Planning is limited to the foreseeable future, while a single strategy is often selected following analysis of various options. Both the strategy and its implementation are reviewed on a set schedule, and small, incremental adjustments are made over the medium term to adhere to fixed targets.

However, this approach doesn't allow for a dynamic, unpredictable environment. Single strategies and limited planning restrict an organisation's ability to effectively respond to new opportunities or threats. Traditional strategic tools and analysis struggle to provide the dynamic insights that underpin competitive advantage, while fixed methodologies restrict organisational agility. Increased business uncertainty further limits organisations' view to the near term as longer-term bets appear too risky, creating a vicious cycle of short-termism.

Many established leadership styles create organisational drag. A growing proportion of the workforce is independent, and many permanent workers are increasingly motivated by leaders who enable career fulfilment. Older 'fire and brimstone' approaches where compliance and punishment drive organisational performance are ceding ground to collaborative methods that inspire and engage human capital to focus on the bigger picture.

Now, trust in leadership has become essential in delivering the strategy. Stephen Covey, author of *The 7 Habits of Highly Effective People* (Simon & Schuster UK, 2013), claimed that "the speed of trust" enables leaders and human capital to work far more efficiently and productively. More trust leads to increased speed and reduced costs, whereas less trust leads to increased suspicion, which in turn decreases speed and increases costs.

Any perception of managers 'juicing' their organisations for individual or shareholder gain at the expense of employees, customers, or the community is likely to result in declining performance and profitability. This is more pronounced in more recent workforce generations who are less influenced by the long-term financial security associated with permanent employment.

As leaders are increasingly visible and subject to much greater scrutiny, influence, integrity, and credibility are replacing hierarchy and seniority as key levers to deliver The Plan.

> Part of Microsoft's recent success can be attributed to Satya Nadella's strong approval ratings compared to his predecessor, whereas the commercial turbulence experienced by Ryanair correlates with CEO Michael O'Leary's reputation with employees.

Impact summary: Delivering The Plan

It is harder for leaders to devise and deliver plans. The scale, speed, and variety of inputs that leaders need to consider is dramatically larger in the digital age, making it harder to differentiate between signals and noise. Increased commercial uncertainty and instability are creating organisational friction, diverting human capital away from key objectives. Traditional strategic models and management approaches are proving ineffective at delivering the results required.

Optimising in the digital age

These impacts fundamentally change how organisations approach The Plan. Plans need to deliver results faster at the same time as mitigating the risks from weakening operational foundations and new disruptive challengers. They need to effectively engage more demanding customers today, while accurately forecasting an increasingly unpredictable tomorrow.

They need to harness a more ambitious and distributed workforce to cope with the increased volume, velocity, and variety of opportunities and challenges. While a one-size approach will obviously not work for all organisations, effective plans and strategies in the digital age share some critical similarities.

Recommendation 1: Adaptive planning

Clarify your purpose

In an increasingly crowded, competitive, and chaotic world where expectations have transformed, a clear, authentic purpose connects all stakeholders to The Plan. For a growing number of consumers and clients, it's a key reason to buy and keep buying. For workers, it provides a key motivation to work hard and strive for more. For investors and shareholders, it establishes market relevance and long-term potential.

Purposeful organisations not only provide strong, clear guidance on why they exist, but they commit to living that purpose every day. A purpose that is pursued wholly and authentically resonates with all relevant audiences, whereas a purpose that is stated but not embraced is quickly recognised and often toxic.

Leaders should first **rediscover and redefine their authentic purpose**. According to Helen Rosethorn, partner at Prophet, a growth and digital transformation firm, leaders need to first conduct a thorough and honest examination of why their organisation really matters to ensure their purpose is rooted in the truth. They must fully commit to enacting their purpose to inspire those around them to do the same. Purpose requires "room to breathe" away from competing business initiatives, giving everyone time to see it, understand it, and engage with it. Finally, people need to be empowered to use it every day. (*'Becoming Purposeful': A Prophet report in collaboration with HR Grapevine, 2018.*)

PwC recommends that leaders focus on authenticity while "preparing for impact", giving up some short-term opportunities to enable long-term adherence to The Plan. They should select talent based on their alignment to purpose, rather than immediate skillset shortages, and bake purpose and values into business rules and decision-making criteria to constantly reinforce the importance of purpose in everything the business does.[26]

Next, ensure The Plan considers the **demands that customers will have tomorrow**, as well as those they have today. Empower key employees to regularly spend time working directly with customers, understanding their hopes and aspirations, constraints and challenges. Involve customers more directly in the planning and strategy process by inviting them to planning sessions. Actively leverage the vast treasure troves of customer data you have or can transparently acquire, while investing in long-term customer relationships. We explore customer-centric approaches in much more detail in *Chapter 7: Positioning for Success.*

Place **customer experience and innovation at the heart of The Plan**. Customer experience, not customer service, is now essential in retaining existing customers and attracting new ones – and demand for better products and services increases the importance of creativity and innovation. To enable this, shorten release cycles and test new iterations or capabilities more often, generating real-time feedback from customers, operations, suppliers, and human capital.

Prioritise worker behaviours and attributes that drive creativity – encouraging and rewarding continuous innovation that delivers exciting experiences. Re-map and measure experiences across all customer journeys, paying particular attention to important interactions away from the point of purchase, making sure that everyone in the organisation understands the importance of engaging relationships across the entire customer lifecycle.

Continuous strategy

Strategic thinking should become an everyday activity. Organisations need to develop a fast, flexible, systematic approach to strategy that underwrites the focus on the big picture while empowering individual autonomy to contribute to, evolve, and deliver it. Create a continuous strategy program to run alongside the annual strategy process, enabling your business to regularly explore new challenges, test new ideas, and implement new approaches without destabilising the broader strategic approach.

Implement a **systematic strategic framework** that embraces and encourages diversity of thought to facilitate innovative solutions on how the strategy is achieved. This framework helps everyone to stay focused and aligned with the mission and strategic objectives while simultaneously adapting the strategy to better fit changing realities. Collectively, this allows the entire organisation to be independently proactive and reactive at the same time, and ensures that everyone pulls in the same direction.

Set up regular **employee strategy forums** with capable individuals from across the business to discuss strategic issues, debate solutions, and prioritise actions. Encourage everyone to provide new ideas to continuously improve on existing approaches, challenge ineffective methodologies, and share relevant market information.

The outputs of this forum can be reviewed by a **strategy board** made up of key members of the senior leadership team and the main board. The strategy board can then list and prioritise issues, steering the employee strategy forum to focus on particular challenges as and when necessary.

Stay alert

Market trends and shocks create opportunities and risks faster than ever before. While organisations must remain focused on their core purpose, they cannot lose sight of the changing realities and risks of running the business from day to day. By constantly listening, understanding trends, and predicting challenges, enterprises can better balance demand for short-term profitability with longer-term sustainability and relevance.

First, ensure that your teams are **connected to the *right* sources of information**. Identify the most appropriate sources and set up filters to screen out as much background noise as possible. Enable teams to focus on the quality not quantity of data, as a surfeit of information creates a poverty of attention.

Set up channel feedback loops and alerts to automate content delivery. Augment insights with data, leveraging Big Data if available, to spot opportunities as well as risks. Focus on the factors that are vital to competitive advantage, separating clear trends from passing fads to ensure that insights are meaningful. There are various decision frameworks online that help businesses do this systematically.

Monitor **the *nature* of disruptions**, not just the disruptors themselves, to identify broader changes that might reshape markets. The internet sowed the seeds of destruction for physical newspapers, and smartphones undermined camera sales. The insights gained will also enable organisations to plan more effectively for the resources they require, be it raw materials or skills and experience – reducing costs and risks while increasing speed.

Encourage decision-makers to spend time with innovators, surround themselves with people who think differently, and **embrace different perspectives** head on. Incentivise key leaders and managers to develop external industry networks, budgeting time and resources to experience different mindsets and ideas. Connect cross-functional teams with capable and candid people within the organisation who are closer to customers or have trusted insights on the day-to-day realities or challenges posed by competitor innovations.

Recommendation summary: Adaptive planning

The Plan must clarify your purpose, providing authentic meaning to engage and inspire more demanding stakeholders. It should include a framework for organisational thinking and acting that maintains this clarity while encouraging creativity and freedom to experiment with different approaches. Finally, it should be built on continuous and high-quality information streams to course-correct based on constantly changing realities.

Recommendation 2: Empowering through distributed autonomy

Build organisational IQ and EQ

Leveraging distributed teams helps leaders to develop sharper and more relevant strategies, stronger ownership and support, and closer alignment and collaboration on organisational objectives. However, before leaders can do this, there needs to be enough strategic capability and competence to effectively deliver The Plan. That means investing in initiatives that develop both organisational (IQ) and emotional intelligence (EQ) to help distributed teams rise to the challenge.

Train key individuals throughout the business to be more strategic. In functional leadership teams, training should not only develop core strategic knowledge and skills, but also focus on understanding and empathy for the wider strategic challenges facing the organisation. Existing corporate strategy leaders are well-placed to lead these initiatives, combining their knowledge of the business and markets with an understanding of the structure and roles of the organisation. This also has the added advantage of visibly involving the wider business in strategy – reinforcing shared ownership and commitment.

Next, set up **horizontal connections between functional units** to drive collaboration on strategy. For example, teams from different business units might work together to answer specific strategic questions for the executive team. This not only encourages innovation as different teams bring fresher thinking and new perspectives to the development of solutions, but it also builds understanding and empathy for the challenges that other functions face.

Organisations can rotate high-potential employees on secondments in different functional areas to enhance cross-functional collaboration and empathy. They can also incentivise workers to set up their own collaborative networks through individual performance objectives.

Finally, create **localised open forum sessions** to discuss and debate strategy. Invite employees, external partners, independent workers, contractors, and key customers. Encourage people to ask questions, participate in debates, and contribute ideas. Directly address misunderstandings and misinterpretations, with examples of how incorrect interpretations (no matter how well-intentioned) distract from the intended strategy. Co-run these sessions with the newly-trained functional strategy leaders, and deliver them across the entire business so everyone can get involved.

Empower distributed ownership

When you give teams' responsibility for choosing the steps that deliver The Plan, it strengthens ownership. In *The Barcelona Way* (Macmillan, 2018), Professor Damian Hughes explains how the power of choice convinces people that they are in control, endowing their actions with a sense of meaning. When people assert that they have authority over their lives, they become motivated. Giving teams more control over their future not only improves the delivery of corporate strategy, but also optimises senior governance, liberating executive teams to focus on the bigger challenges ahead.

Ensure that your **business and functional leaders develop and deliver their own strategy** with their teams and make them collectively accountable for behaviours and execution. While these plans should be fully aligned to the corporate strategy and purpose defined by the executive leadership team, the power of this approach lies in business and functional leaders choosing their own path to deliver it.

Ensure that teams **self-review** their progress on a regular basis and develop their own specific results-oriented metrics alongside the wider organisational goals. Relate reward and recognition to the achievement of both functional and company goals. Empower teams to self-correct any deviations from The Plan, reinforcing ownership and accountability of the strategy.

The **CEO and executive team should actively review and remain involved** in business and functional strategy, but step back to enable teams to design, develop, and deliver their own plan. Executive leadership teams should focus on a few simple, critical corporate goals while guarding against unintentionality. They should ensure there is a clear link between functional strategies and the corporate strategy, then empower teams to resolve misalignment within and between these plans. This approach delivers strong oversight and influence, enabling senior leaders to step in to re-prioritise and coordinate actions during more challenging times.

Underwrite strategic clarity

Invest in improved communication systems and frameworks that provide a clear line of sight between the organisation's mission, business and functional strategies, and individual performance. Then, continuously reinforce this connection through regular and powerful interventions that protect the organisation against deviation from the strategy.

Start by **synthesising your purpose and corporate strategy in a concise way** that is both easy to communicate and understand. Paint the picture to help everyone across the organisation (including outsourced partners and independent workers) fully understand why you do what you do, where you are going, and the behaviours that will get you there. Regularly assess the quality of comprehension and alignment, using feedback to update and reinforce key messages while simultaneously reducing the danger of misunderstandings and misinterpretation.

Deliver clarity by **repetitively reinforcing strategic objectives**. England football manager Sir Alf Ramsey, whose team won the World Cup in 1966, attributed the secret of great coaching and getting players to fully understand his vision to "constant repetition to get the message home" (*The Barcelona Way*). Reinforce The Plan and strategy at every opportunity, printing it on everything from achievement plans to computer load screens to monthly town halls. To help these messages get digested by everyone involved, use spaced learning to break content into smaller, more memorable chunks within single learning events. For example, if your organisation has three core corporate objectives, launch and communicate these separately as well as together.

Create a simple but **consistent performance framework** that ties everyone's performance objectives to the mission and vision. Intel invented Objective and Key Results (OKRs), which Google has co-opted to achieve stellar results.[27] OKRs translate the strategy and objectives for teams and organisations into tangible, measurable goals – helping workers see how they are contributing to the mission and vision. Foxtel (an Australian TV provider) leveraged 'Achievement Plans' that clearly map business and functional goals and metrics to strategic objectives. Enterprise systems such as Weekdone and Betterworks can help you digitise this approach.

Recommendation summary: Distributed autonomy

The volume and complexity of change – combined with the increased importance of purpose, innovation, and experience – means that senior leaders cannot deliver plans on their own. Instead, leaders should distribute autonomy across the organisation while continually providing the strategic clarity to maintain focus. They should invest in the capability, tools, and frameworks to empower their teams to take strategic ownership, liberating themselves from the tactical so they can focus on the big picture.

Recommendation 3: Build deeper organisational trust and belief

Commit to the long term

Organisations should demonstrate their commitment to the big picture – sometimes at the expense of short-term profitability. By understanding investors' appetite for risk over their venture time horizon, leaders can agree multi-year timeframes for value creation while working closely with them to develop and align corporate governance guidelines. Set expectations with shareholders that short-term underperformance can be tolerated and even expected if it helps longer-term value creation.

> Singapore's sovereign wealth fund GIC maintains a publicly stated 20-year horizon for value creation.[28]

Work with investors to fight the 'Tyranny of Short-termism'[29] and quarterly capitalism. Collaborate with boards and shareholders to define how long-term value creation is measured.

Dominic Barton, global managing partner of McKinsey & Company, and Mark Wiseman, former president and CEO of the Canada Pension Plan Investment Board, recommend focusing on metrics like ten-year 'economic value added', R&D efficiency, patent pipelines and multi-year return on capital investments.[30]

While the fast-paced digital age increases the importance of short-term metrics to empower agility, long-term indicators are essential to safeguard market relevance and sustainable growth.

Within the organisation, openly demonstrate a commitment to long-term value creation. **Reallocate cash reserves and resources** away from parts of the business with diminishing returns into parts of the business that represent the future. Evolve executive roles to ensure that resources are given to higher value creation initiatives and avoid the doom loop of investing in 'what we've always done'. Update the organisation's reward philosophy to incentivise long-term value over short-term opportunism by implementing deferred compensation or long-term stock models.

Fight the fear

Fear paralyses organisations. Fear of change, fear of the unknown, and fear of failure all create friction and prevent organisations from effectively delivering The Plan. Instead, organisations need their workers to believe in the future so they can deliver in the present. Leaders throughout organisations play a critical role in creating an environment that keeps everyone focused on their intended objectives.

Leaders must drive clarity. By being open and honest, those working for them are reassured that there is nothing to hide. Through regularly communicating successes, opportunities, threats, *and* failures, leaders create an environment where objectives are reinforced and mistakes aren't hidden. Leaders must address negative behaviours that derail The Plan, especially when those behaviours lead to short-term gains at the expense of long-term value. Leaders should constantly demonstrate the integrity that encourages junior talent to contribute to the success of the business.

Next, leaders should **proactively remove ambiguity**. This means constantly guarding against misunderstandings and misinterpretations of the strategy, and seeking out and addressing unintentionality at all levels. Simultaneously, they should create an environment that inspires confidence and belief in a clear collective plan and address the institutional inertia that prevents human capital from trying new ideas.

Finally, target and incentivise capable members of the business to become

internal influencers and ambassadors. Focus on relationships that build cross-functional empathy, understanding, and knowledge-sharing. Prioritise parts of the organisation furthest from the centre, engaging critical members of the workforce that may have previously received less attention. Don't ignore external partners and independent workers either – they play an equally critical role in delivering The Plan and can be both critical sources of innovation and pivotal to the customer experience.

Incentivise trust, collaboration, and curiosity

Encourage the behaviours and actions that reinforce collective trust in The Plan. For example, excessive executive pay deals or inconsistently managed behaviours can quickly destroy any organisational trust built elsewhere. Instead, leaders must prioritise, measure and reward the right values and behaviours for everyone in the organisation, applying them consistently to *everyone* from the CEO down. While the next chapter on culture explores the role of values and behaviours in greater detail, leaders should incentivise their organisation to constantly prioritise the big picture.

To help break down operating silos, organisations would do well to **reward combined initiatives** such as cross-selling, talent retention, or inter-functional strategic programmes. Beyond rewards targeted at individual performance and behaviours, incentivise the results of collaboration, particularly between – rather than just within – business units. Publicly recognise initiatives that benefit the company as a whole, especially if they come with short-term disadvantages to individuals or teams.

Additionally, seek ways to **incentivise constructive curiosity** across the entire distributed workforce. Reward the exploration or development of new ideas and solutions that help deliver The Plan, or positive challenges to the status quo. While organisations shouldn't reward workers for errors or defiance, encouraging contributions from across the business helps workers focus on the wider perspective and contribute to collective success.

Recommendation summary: Organisational trust

The success of The Plan is now predicated on the strength of organisational trust. When customers trust an organisation, they are more likely to buy and remain loyal. This in turn creates the conditions for shareholders to invest and remain patient, which in turn empowers human capital to create the game-changing offerings that customers want to buy. However, trust starts within the organisation, requiring leaders to create a business environment that addresses commercial uncertainty while delivering deeper confidence and conviction in long-term value creation.

The Plan

IMPACT OF FORCES

I1. Demand for faster, fresher, more adaptable strategies	*I2.* Plans must deliver wider, more challenging outcomes	*I3.* Delivering The Plan is harder
Product and services lifecycle shortening • Demand for more innovative features more frequently • Maturity phase compressing • External specialists accelerate development and delivery of higher-quality offerings	**Different success criteria** • Customer focus on purpose, values, and ethics • Shareholders motivated by long-term relevance and sustainability • Higher workforce expectations	**More complexity** • Navigate more distractions • Harder to forecast market conditions • Staying strategically aligned is more complicated
Changing commercial certainties • Global supply chains disrupted • Cost of doing business increasing • Unpredictability of fossil fuel price and supply	**Customer experience and innovation are key strategic drivers** • Customer-centric replaces product-centric • All customer experiences matter • Customer interactions at time and place of their choosing	**Increased organisational friction** • Magnified misunderstandings and misinterpretations • Greater deviation from The Plan • Poor behaviours amplified
Traditional plans less competitive • Reduced need for intermediaries • Greater transparency of margins above industry standard • New analytics transformed value of business data	**Staying ahead of the curve essential to relevance** • More accurately predict demand • Understand demand before customers know it themselves • Constant innovation required	**Shifting realities for leaders** • Traditional strategy models less effective • Traditional people management creates drag • Organisational trust increasingly critical

RECOMMENDATIONS ACTIVATE

ACTIVATE

R1. Adaptive planning	*R2.* Empowering through distributed autonomy	*R3.* Build deeper organisational trust and belief
Clarify your purpose • Rediscover and redefine authentic purpose • Consider demands of tomorrow as well as today • Experience and innovation at the heart of The Plan	**Build organisational IQ and EQ** • Train key individuals • Build horizontal connections between functions • Localised open forum sessions	**Commit to the long term** • Work with investors to fight quarterly capitalism • Reallocate roles and update reward
Continuous strategy • Systematic strategic framework • Regular employee strategy forum • Strategy board review	**Empower distributed ownership** • Functional leaders develop and deliver own strategy • Self-review and self-correction • CEO and executive team actively review	**Fight the fear** • Leaders drive transparency • Proactively remove ambiguity • Appoint internal influencers and ambassadors
Stay alert • Connect to right sources of information • Monitor the nature of disruptions • Embrace different perspectives	**Underwrite strategic clarity** • Clear and concise purpose and corporate strategy • Repetitively reinforce objectives • Consistent performance framework	**Incentivise trust, collaboration and curiosity** • Reward combined initiatives • Incentivise constructive curiosity

CHAPTER 5

Culture

Organisational culture is a set of shared assumptions that inform how an organisation behaves. Culture guides the workforce on how to act in different work situations, be it dealing with a challenging customer request, collaborating with colleagues, escalating a burgeoning commercial problem, or proposing a radical but risky new idea. According to Frances Frei and Anne Morriss at Harvard Business School, culture essentially tells employees what to do when the CEO isn't in the room, which is of course most of the time.[1]

Culture includes the values and behaviours that "contribute to the unique social and psychological environment of an organisation".[2] It's shown in the way that organisations conduct business and treat their employees, customers, and the wider community. It exists separately from The Plan but plays a fundamental role in how The Plan is delivered. It defines the extent to which freedom is allowed in decision-making, new idea development, and personal expression. It outlines how power and information flow through the hierarchy. It impacts how "committed employees are towards collective objectives, influencing happiness, engagement, and the productivity of human capital". (ibid)

It also exists whether you like it or not. The internal IM conversations, the team meetings, the chat in the bar after work, the holiday request process, the conversations around the board table. These are all part of the everyday human capital experiences that create an organisation's culture.

Why should leaders care?

There is plenty of evidence suggesting that cultivating a positive culture around shared values gives companies a significant advantage over their competitors. In *The Hungry Spirit* (Random House, 1998), Charles Handy stated that individuals who perceive that their very human need for meaning and purpose is being met at work exhibit higher levels of performance and put in greater discretionary effort. James L. Heskett goes further in *The Culture Cycle: How to Shape the Unseen Force that Transforms Performance* (Pearson FT Press, 2011), saying that beyond simply work output, culture is a powerful driver of engagement, which leads to better financial performance. In other words, happy, engaged workers are more productive workers.

Peter Drucker reputedly claimed that "culture could eat strategy for breakfast", such is the importance of positive culture in the success of an enterprise. As money is the language of business, it's worth quantifying exactly how much culture impacts the bottom line. The University of Warwick's Department of Economics found that happy workers are 12% more productive than average ones, while unhappy workers are 10% less productive.[3]

In fact, according to Gallup, unhappy employees already cost American business over $300 billion each year.[4] The *Harvard Business Review* reported that low-level engagement results in a 33% decrease in operating income and an 11% decrease in earnings growth, whereas companies with high-level engagement see a 19% increase in operating income and a 28% increase in earnings growth.[5]

Other studies support these conclusions. Ontario's Queen's School of Business and Gallup reported that disengaged workers had 37% higher absenteeism, 49% more accidents, and 60% more errors and defects in their work. In organisations with low employee engagement scores, there was 18% lower productivity, 16% lower profitability, 37% lower job growth, and 65% lower share price.[6]

However, a strong culture can also deliver unprecedented success beyond the balance sheet.

> The All Blacks, New Zealand's national rugby union team, have become the world's most successful sporting franchise based in part on their culture. Their mantra "Better People Make Better All Blacks" helped them rebuild their team following a poor run of form and propelled them to international dominance. Since the introduction of world rankings in 2003, they have ranked first 87% of the time and since 2011, they've boasted an 89% win record.[7]

Put simply, developing and maintaining a genuine, positive culture delivers improved performance *and* productivity.

Impact of the forces

Despite mounting evidence over the past 30 years, many leaders still don't consider cultivating a positive culture as an important tool to shape their company's success. Some organisations are unwilling to invest in initiatives without quantifiable returns on investment (ROIs) or tangible short-term financial benefits. Others remain unconvinced by the evidence, while a minority seem to accept poor culture as a necessary by-product of previous success. Despite its proven value, culture has often been de-prioritised in favour of tactical initiatives that appear easier to deliver and simpler to measure.

However, the digital world magnifies the role of culture in delivering commercial value and growth. Evolving stakeholder expectations highlight the importance of engaged workforces to connect and retain customers. Organisational collaboration and trust are key drivers of speed, agility, and innovation. As workforce characteristics change and talent seeks greater career fulfilment, aligning values and behaviours in an organisation has become essential in improving performance. As such, culture is now a critical lever in driving profitability.

Impact 4: Culture has become an essential leadership tool

Positive culture is a key driver of competitive advantage

Author, speaker, and organisational consultant Simon Sinek claimed: "People don't buy what you do; they buy why you do it".[8] His advice to companies is not to sell to people what they have, but to sell to people who believed what the company believed. Customers, investors, employees, and candidates are increasingly motivated by 'the why' rather than 'the what', making a company's culture key in connecting with all their stakeholders. It provides tangible evidence of an organisation's values, beliefs, and alignment to their stated purpose, becoming a key litmus test of authenticity.

In fact, culture is now critical in creating exceptional customer experiences and loyalty. The workforce (full-time, independent, and outsourced) is an increasingly visible and important interface between an organisation and its customers. Subsequently, culture has become essential in finding, engaging, and inspiring this human capital to deliver the customer experiences that make the difference between a loyal customer and a disgruntled antagonist.

Unsurprisingly, happy, engaged workers deliver better customer experiences than unhappy, disengaged ones. In their 'State of the American Workplace' report, Gallup reported that engaged employees are more likely to improve customer relationships – with a resulting 20% increase in sales.[9]

Positive cultures are also essential for innovation. As consumer expectations increase, organisations have to constantly find new ways to excite and delight their customers, keeping them engaged and loyal. Consequently, an open, supportive culture where innovation is fostered and encouraged (and failure is acknowledged as a necessary step to success) has a clear commercial advantage over closed environments that restrict creativity and punish mistakes.

Google encouraged employees to spend 20% of their time working on ideas they thought would most benefit Google, creating huge successes such as Gmail, GoogleMaps, and AdSense.[10] Likewise, Intuit CEO Brad Smith suggests that success comes from leaders "removing barriers to innovation and getting out of the way".[11]

Culture underpins speed, consistency, and risk management

Moreover, culture is key to enabling speed and agility. As windows of opportunity narrow, companies with good cultures experience better information-sharing and problem-solving. This results in the identification of more solutions, better preparation for competitor activity, and enhanced reaction times to faster-moving threats.

As customer attention spans and patience drops, culture empowers workers to resolve customer issues on the spot or quickly offer solutions that increase customer lifetime value. As businesses become ever more reliant on external specialists and interdisciplinary collaboration, culture is one of the few tools that can unify teams through shared values and behaviours.

Culture plays an even bigger role in delivering consistency. According to *McKinsey Quarterly* (July 2017) on "Culture for a digital age", organisations are being forced to find new ways to respond to 'best-in-class' online and offline user demand, react swiftly to enquiries, customise products and services seamlessly, and provide easy access to the information that customers need, when they need it.[12]

Culture has become the glue that unifies all parts of the organisation to deliver these demanding expectations, helping workforces to mobilise around integrated customer touchpoints. What's more, culture helps to align day-to-day tactical decisions with The Plan, enabling reliable customer experiences to be delivered autonomously and independently by different parts of the business.

Good cultures also help to balance risk-taking. These days, organisations are moving faster and more decisively to capitalise on opportunities and respond to threats. However, these actions come with elevated risks, as businesses make more decisions, quicker, and in uncertain commercial environments.

As organisations get closer to customers, positive cultures reduce the risk of experimentation and deliver more relevant solutions. It encourages innovation in line with The Plan, rather than innovation for innovation's sake, and assists in managing risk, guiding individuals on when to disrupt, when to accelerate, and when to stop. It is a key risk moderator, enabling businesses to accelerate or decelerate their activity in line with changing market dynamics.

The diminishing effectiveness of traditional performance management

Culture is now filling the void left by weakening approaches to human capital performance. As workforces become more multi-generational, less dependent on long-term permanent employment, and increasingly comprised of independent workers, traditional human capital management approaches are not as effective at getting human capital to perform.

The one-size-fits-all annualised performance review is a clear example of this. Often taking a secretive top-down approach, a limited number of senior employees determine yearly performance ratings and rewards. Operating separately from the natural rhythm of the business, these processes do not support the ongoing course corrections required for a faster-paced world. In fact, they disengage workers looking for continuous feedback, ongoing coaching, and more personalised career development. As such, these reviews often result in the opposite of their intended effect – alienating employees and suppressing performance.

In addition, deferred career fulfilment models are not attractive to a growing proportion of the workforce. Recent generations entering the job market are not as prepared as previous generations to sacrifice near-term career fulfilment for the unguaranteed chance of distant success. Partnership models favoured by many professional services companies are less attractive to employees, who are instead looking for career experiences, meaning, and fulfilment in the here and now. It is increasingly likely that organisations which rely on junior talent sacrificing their time, social lives, and freedom because 'that what the senior leaders did' will struggle to keep a critical and growing proportion of their workforce engaged.

Finally, short-term financial incentives are proving less effective at driving sustained performance. While money can and does motivate people to work, evidence suggests that performance-related bonuses don't deliver corresponding performance improvements. According to Don Rheem, author of *Thrive By Design: The Neuroscience That Drives High-Performance Cultures* (ForbesBooks, 2017), purely financial rewards are extrinsic. Money satisfies but has very little impact on behaviour and performance. As workers look for meaning and purpose in their careers, they become more motivated by intrinsic rewards such as recognition, impact, and respect.[13]

Impact summary: Key leadership tool

Culture is increasingly key to connecting with all stakeholders. Strong cultures deliver improvements to customer experience, product innovation, risk management and commercial agility. They underpin better workforce performance, which in turn strengthens the underlying investment for shareholders. Conversely, weak cultures magnify the challenges that organisations face, increasing organisational friction and undermining The Plan. As traditional performance management approaches deliver diminishing returns, a strong, positive culture is essential to sustainable success.

Impact 5: Engagement is harder to win and easier to lose

Cultural authenticity is increasingly important

Just like consumers, workforces have lost trust in established organisations. Instead, their engagement is increasingly driven by shared alignment in values, honesty, and sustainability. A powerful, ethical, and authentic culture is essential in attracting, engaging, and inspiring critical human capital to perform.

Workers are increasingly motivated by alignment between an organisation's purpose and their own. They expect to share in an organisation's culture, proactively participating and contributing to collective values and behaviours while having the freedom to constructively challenge the status quo. Employees are less likely to replace their personal values and behaviours or conform to a predefined set of attributes – 'fixing themselves' to fit in.

> Even though onboarding approaches found at Google ('Nooglers') and Ted Baker ('Tedification') drive cultural consistency, they replace rather than share values, leaving organisations exposed to cultural inconsistencies when pressures mount.

Importantly, culture cannot be bought. While extrinsic displays of 'cultural cool' have become popular, people are motivated by the intrinsic attributes that align and inspire them with a greater shared cause. Workers are more discerning and discriminating when viewing organisational culture (especially Generations Y and Z) and less likely to be influenced by gimmicks.

Indoor slides, private chefs, games rooms, or over-the-top parties can work well when they genuinely and continuously reflect an organisation's values and principles. However, by themselves, they don't equal good corporate culture, and conversely are often considered contrived or fake if they don't accurately reflect reality.

These days, workers place far more significance on honesty and transparency.

Candidates want to see opportunities talked about and reviewed within a relatable context to understand the true experience of working at an organisation. Employees want open, honest, and direct communication from their leaders regardless of the topic, situation, or context. And third-party suppliers and independent workers want to better understand the real challenges they are solving, so they can use their specialist talents to add genuine value. As human capital increasingly prizes honesty, glossy projections of unrealistic perfection or the restriction of key information significantly impacts engagement.

Constantly and consistently reflected

Both customers and workers expect organisations to live and breathe their culture in every interaction. They want consistent, high-quality experiences that reflect and reinforce an organisation's stated values and behaviours. They are increasingly conscious of cultural inconsistencies and intolerant when any discrepancies are not addressed.

Both consumers and clients expect organisations to demonstrate their purpose, values, and behaviours in all of their day-to-day activities. Potential customers expect their first interaction to powerfully emphasise the stated culture. Existing customers want to see a reinforcement of the culture they have aligned with every time they connect with their chosen vendor, no matter which part of the business they're interacting with. This is especially true of B2B organisations that have many touchpoints and interactions over the course of the client lifetime.

Workers expect culture to be genuinely reflected at every stage of their career with a business. They expect continuity between and within the various stages of the talent lifecycle, not just while they're being recruited. Culture has become a reflection of leadership – as much as a reflection of business, with human capital now expecting consistent and congruent standards of leadership across all parts of the organisation. Any inconsistencies are rapidly shared, both inside and outside the company.

Finally, *all* human capital expects to be treated professionally and respectfully, regardless of each individual's role or potential value. Recruitment processes where unsuccessful candidates are left waiting for weeks or receive bland, generic responses significantly undermine a company's reputation. Likewise, career development opportunities limited to a chosen few quickly disengages essential, if not 'high-potential', talent. External suppliers and independent partners expect to be treated as valuable equals, not second-class citizens. As the balance of power shifts away from employers towards workers, companies can no longer ignore the experiences of unsuccessful candidates, external partners, or rank-and-file employees.

Culture much more visible

The plethora of social media and multiple information exchange platforms mean that organisational culture – warts and all – is incredibly visible. More and more workers are turning to independent like-minded peers for authentic insights into companies, circumventing corporate attempts to broadcast a 'glossy' representation of culture. In fact, candidates now have instant access to up-to-the-minute organisational information from so many sources that they can screen a company as much as a company screens them.

For example, companies and managers are rated much like Airbnb or Amazon sellers. Detailed commercial performance is discussed and dissected, the ethics and social responsibility of firms are judged, and CEO performance is scrutinised.

> Glassdoor has built a database of over 8 million company reviews including leadership/management ratings, salary reports, and workplace insights.[14] Dedicated websites such as Kununu, Great Place to Work, Vault, and Comparably offer structured and searchable ratings on a range of company or manager variables. The anonymous messaging app Memo allows employees to share any opinions with their co-workers and with registered users outside the company network.[15]

Independent peer-review sites also provide a huge depth and breadth of insight.

> The pay-per-hire site Indeed allows candidates to review companies based on job security and advancement. Comparably measures awards, gender, and diversity scores. TheJobCrowd measures environmental awareness and responsibility. LinkedIn, Twitter, and Facebook enable direct communication with peer networks, allowing candidates to crowdsource specific answers and cross-reference them for accuracy.

Finally, inconsistencies in organisational culture are much more exposed. As human capital readily gains access to independent information and shares it more frequently, the difference between a published set of behaviours and those that organisations *actually* reward becomes far more transparent. Any disparities manifest as a hollow set of principles, and this impacts on talent acquisition, retention, customer engagement, and investor confidence. As more discrepancies are shared, it becomes harder to attract, engage, and retain critical talent.

Impact summary: Engagement harder to win and easier to lose

Human capital expectations of culture have evolved, placing greater emphasis on authenticity, shared values, and shared success. Culture needs to be consistently and constantly reflected throughout both customer and talent lifecycles. At the same time, workers have a much clearer view on the cultural realities of working at a business, making any inconsistencies more transparent and potentially toxic.

Impact 6: Organisations are dependent on an increasingly distributed and diverse workforce

The non-permanent workforce is increasingly important

As the proportion of permanent workers decreases, organisations are becoming reliant on their non-permanent workforce. External suppliers and partners now interact directly with customers, fulfil essential parts of the value chain, and help shape products and services. Businesses must now extend their culture to include every part of their operation so that they can capitalise on opportunities, deliver consistent and high-quality experiences, and develop better offerings.

Agility and responsiveness depend on every part of the supply chain reacting rapidly and effectively to change. Innovation and problem-solving rely on internal and external employees sharing information and collaborating effectively. Customer loyalty is subject to consistent positive experiences at every stage of the customer journey, whether they are interacting with a full-time employee (FTE), a partner, or a contractor.

In addition, external partners are a vital source of information and innovation. Third-party suppliers offer broader, richer skillsets, having been exposed to different situations and commercial objectives. Specialist suppliers have deeper subject matter expertise and are better connected to relevant market intelligence, accelerating their ability to solve industry-specific challenges. Greater knowledge and familiarity with the latest technology enables third parties to deliver more objective advice, empowering business to make much faster, better-informed investment decisions.

However, external suppliers and providers are also a growing source of risk. Workforces are only as strong as their weakest link, and organisations are reliant on their partners operating to the same standards, values, and behaviours as they do. This is rising in importance as customers and clients don't differentiate between FTEs, flexible resources, or external partners, and expect the same quality of experience from outsourced parts of the supply chain, regardless of the supplier processes, infrastructure, and systems that support them.

Cultural consistency is harder to maintain

Cultures now have to address a wider, more complicated, and more fluid set of motivations. As many individuals and teams operate virtually, there are fewer interpersonal opportunities for people to share and align behaviours and values. As more and more human capital operates outside permanent employment, traditional cultural engagement mechanisms are becoming less effective.

Workforces are increasingly culturally dynamic and diverse. Established cultural boundaries are breaking, as teams and organisational structures are reconfigured and re-blended around projects and results – not functions and tasks. There is an increasing mix of generations and nationalities, operating out of more geographically disbursed locations. There is increased movement within businesses as a greater proportion of employees at different career stages actively pursue broader career experiences. And there are more external contributors, with more varied values that they want to share.

At the same time, people have fewer opportunities to deepen their cultural alignment. As they spend less time as permanent employees, their exposure to mutual values and behaviours is limited. Fewer individuals work out of fixed employment locations, and fewer teams are co-located in the same workspace. Human capital is now distributed over a greater variety of locations, operating from home, shared workspaces, and coffee shops. Some are even increasing their exposure to the different and potentially conflicting cultures, values, and behaviours of other enterprises, sharing workplaces in co-location facilities such as WeWork.

As a result, the established cultural practices built up around traditional employment are less effective at empowering shared values and behaviours. There are fewer opportunities to build networks and relationships that were traditionally formed over time through corridor conversations, impromptu introductions, or after-work drinks. Furthermore, there is less 'in person' communication as a greater proportion of communication takes place online. This is altering the nature of work relationships, making it harder to build rich, personal connections. What's more, many existing corporate collaboration platforms exclude non-permanent members of the team, which has big implications and constraints as workforces become more fragmented.

Impact summary: Distributed workforce

The distinction between the permanent and non-permanent, remote and onsite, multi-generational and multi-stage segments of the workforce is blurring. All human capital in an organisation's supply chain has become equally important in achieving results. However, sharing and aligning behaviours and values has become more difficult as teams become more diverse and disbursed.

Optimising in the digital age

Culture has become an indispensable ingredient in the delivery of brilliant customer experiences, game-changing innovation, and greater commercial agility. It is core to reaching and unifying more demanding, diverse, and distributed talent. It is fundamental to improving commercial performance, guiding human capital to proactively do the right things, rather than reactively stopping them from doing the wrong things. Culture is an enabler that delivers clear competitive advantage.

As such, culture is now a strategic imperative for any leadership team. The accelerating forces of change and resulting impacts require organisations to re-prioritise culture – raising its importance to the same level as planning and strategy, if not higher. Leaders must dedicate time and resources to shaping culture deliberately and continuously, driving high standards to constantly reinforce essential behaviours. They must create a self-regulating environment where workers collectively own and shape the culture, holding each other accountable for performance.

Recommendation 4: Build intrinsic strength

Distil your authentic identity

Cultures are stronger and more resilient when they're linked to fundamental, intrinsic behaviours and principles. Deep-seated, natural values enable clear decision-making under pressure and unify organisations against external threats without them needing to be constantly reinforced or micromanaged.

To enable this, a **culture audit** can help leaders truly understand the attributes that make their organisation tick. This audit should draw on multiple sources of information over an extended timeframe. Just conducting an annual employee survey will not supply the breadth and depth of insights needed. Instead, an audit can evaluate how leaders act under pressure, as well as the external perceptions of customers, clients, partners, candidates, and competitors (if possible). The audit should help identify the values and behaviours that have made your organisation successful, as well as the ones that have got in the way.

Audits can be **scaled to fit capacity, budgets, and timescales**. A regular questionnaire can provide basic awareness of key behaviours and values, while a more thorough approach by external specialists or internal audit departments can deliver deeper insights across a range of factors. Of course, the more thorough the audit, the more comprehensive the insights. Be careful to anonymise inputs, as depending on your culture, there may be a fear of retaliation, which will distort your findings. Importantly, be bold, asking tough questions even if the potential answers make for uncomfortable reading.

Finally, **honestly and openly review the results**. While the audit will help to uncover the intrinsic behaviours that empower success, it will simultaneously uncover the behaviours and values that derail it. There is little benefit in defining and accentuating the good if the not-so-good is ignored, denied, or allowed to fester. Candidly share both positive and negative insights across the business, collaborating with teams to develop a prioritised plan that deals with both.

Recalibrate culture

Next, blend the crucial essence of your past with the essential attributes of your future. Using the audit results, **clearly define and articulate the authentic values and behaviours that made your business successful**. Embrace your idiosyncrasies, eccentricities, habits, and foibles as unique parts of your organisation's personality.

For example, if your quintessential character is suits not jeans, Earl Grey not IPA, quiz nights not party nights, ensure that your cultural definitions and interventions reflect that. Customise these characterisations to ensure they resonate with employees. Too many organisations miss the opportunity to truly engage their workforce by promoting bland, interchangeable, and uninspiring values that end up becoming meaningless.

Powerful cultures are also built on the values that address the new demands of the digital age. For example, critical reasoning, the ability to unravel complex issues or to enable distributed collaboration are increasingly essential behaviours. **Augment your natural behaviours and ethics with the essential values** that support your updated purpose and strategy. A more detailed review of these attributes is explored in *Chapter 9: Leveraging Human Capital*.

Finally, **align these collective values to your purpose**, creating a clear line of sight between indispensable behaviours and commercial results. When employees clearly understand *how* values and behaviours deliver the mission, they hold themselves and their peers more accountable for meeting them. Paint the picture of how your culture delivers commercial success.

For example, if an organisation has a goal to grow its customer base and one of its core values is "be courageous", then admitting errors to customers to increase loyalty or pursuing untested opportunities in new markets articulates how bravery increases customer numbers.

Genuine, long-term investment

To deliver on culture's undoubted potential, workforces have to live and breathe their organisation's values every day. However, too many cultures are rendered impotent by disenfranchised workers who experience the gap between what organisations say and what they do. Leaders play a vital role in repositioning culture within their business, re-establishing its importance, and inspiring long-term and ongoing commitment through their own behaviours.

To begin with, **CEOs and executive teams have to relaunch their recalibrated culture** to their business. The workforce needs to see that the most senior people in the organisation believe in and are committed long-term to the culture. This cannot be devolved to HR or other functions – it must be a core accountability of senior leadership teams. Reframe the conversation by articulating the impact on commercial performance from a positive culture aligned with company purpose, while simultaneously communicating the risks of not investing.

Next, **set and measure behavioural goals**. Simply stating values does not translate to improved performance – values must live and breathe in all behaviours and interactions within a business and with its customers. Sometimes called 'keystone behaviours'[16], these patterns of acting are just as important to measure and reward as tactical or operational goals. Establish the metrics that measure your key behaviours and ensure that leaders regularly assess their teams, holding them accountable for any remedial actions. Crucially, to emphasise shared commitment, all leaders should be subject to the same behavioural goals as employees and be held equally accountable.

Finally, budget for **ongoing culture investments**. Culture needs to be continuously reinforced, protected, and evolved, so it's as much a part of operational expenditure as capital expenditure. Budget for regular small, meaningful, everyday interventions that inspire constant commitment, rather than large, glitzy annualised events that are quickly forgotten. Activities should directly promote positive culture. For example, try introducing a regularly updated, interactive tool that enables employees to deeply engage with culture material through quizzes and competitions, deepening their knowledge and alignment.[17]

Recommendation summary: Build intrinsic strength

Powerful cultures are built on authenticity. Seek to understand the core values and behaviours that made your organisation successful in the first place, where necessary augmenting them with values and behaviours essential in the digital age. Align these strengths to your reinvigorated plan, and hold everyone accountable while committing to long-term, ongoing investment.

Recommendation 5: Intentional culture

Constant, clear, prescriptive

Once your recalibrated culture has been launched, provide the **next layer of detail** that supports your core values, helping human capital to apply culture in the real world. Too often, organisations assume that once workers understand their organisation's values, everything else will magically fall into place. However, having a value like Nike's "evolve immediately" could leave many workers confused about how to apply it every day.

Instead, providing crystal-clear guidance reduces ambiguity, making it far easier for people to live the right values and behaviours.

Chris Humphrey and Emma Macdonald, authors of *Culture by Design* (Cranfield University School of Management, 2018), attribute Disney's consistent customer experience and sustained commercial success to their small but defined set of standards that give additional clarity and guidance to employees.[18]

Humphrey and Macdonald also advocate a **priority level** for those standards, so workers can act quickly when there is a potential conflict.

At Disney, the safety standard trumps courtesy, enabling Disney employees to shout at customers for doing something dangerous (Ibid). This gives workforces much greater clarity in how to uphold and apply the values that are critical to their organisation.

To deliver this, ensure that your **values and additional guidance are regularly communicated** to drive the message home. For example, core values should be communicated in every information cascade, in company-wide emails, and on auto-signatures. Additional guidance and standards should be reinforced at town hall meetings, manager 1-2-1s, and in updated performance management reviews. Ensure this guidance is extended to external partners and independent workers to drive consistency across the distributed workforce.

Proactive communication

Adopt a deliberate and structured approach to proactively and effectively share your culture. Using both online and offline communication channels, authentically express your cultural vision to customers, candidates, and workers, leveraging your extended workforce to spread the word.

Encourage continuous transparency, regularly acknowledging and acting on the issues that matter to your workforce. Enterprises thrive on honesty and transparency, both of which are essential to the success of culture. Set up mechanisms to regularly and consistently share official news to extended workforces. Ensure that communications are clear, united, and honest. To be accessible, host regular, open, all-company meetings (where appropriate), listening and respectfully debating any questions or concerns. Ensure that your collaboration technology can reach all essential human capital inside and outside your business, and encourage leaders to proactively engage with their teams' challenges.

Show, rather than tell, audiences about your culture. Develop content and information that demonstrates what your culture is and why it matters. Show customers your employees in real situations, and create stories and narratives that authentically reflect how the organisation lives its values. Build on your history while evolving traditions that encapsulate your ethos, creating positive 'rites of passage' that convey a distinct personality and give audiences something unique to discuss and share.

Incentivise your workforce to create and share their own authentic experiences. Ensure that all human capital understands the stories that genuinely reflect the culture – and encourage them to add their own personal versions. Seek out stories from part-time or remote employees, as well as trusted external partners.

Encourage your people to share their stories to their own online and offline networks. Good posts will showcase your true values to external customers and candidates. Even the not-so-good posts enable you to quickly identify issues before they fester and earn credibility for the company's transparency in the process.

Uncork culture

Ensure that your refreshed culture can travel the length and breadth of your entire organisation. Adopt a talent-centric approach to update existing operational processes, systems, and practices. This will create consistent and congruent experiences while removing unintended bottlenecks and barriers.

Update all people processes to create **integrated and complementary experiences across the talent lifecycle**. Traditionally, operational people processes have been developed as separate, independent programmes that deliver different (and sometimes conflicting) experiences. Instead, redesign the employment experience around the journeys that human capital takes, updating and aligning cultural interventions along the way to drive quality and consistency (for more on this, see *Chapter 9: Leveraging Human Capital*).

Ensure that your **existing people infrastructure supports your updated values**. Reconfigure or upgrade the enterprise software that delivers performance management to support ongoing course corrections and continuous feedback. Update reward mechanisms to incentivise innovation and collaboration. Configure systems to deliver faster, more personalised communication to candidates, employees, and independent workers.

Finally, **retrain all leaders** in their role of supporting culture. Culture fails quickest when leaders don't subscribe to or demonstrate the values, beliefs, and behaviours that an organisation claims to have. In addition to the behavioural goals already mentioned, retrain all leaders on the value of culture and the techniques to support and protect it within their teams.

Recommendation summary: Intentional culture

Leaders cannot sit back and wait for cultural improvements to happen organically. The forces reshaping the modern world are so fast and disruptive that culture must be proactively and continuously shaped. It's imperative that leaders guide their culture with the same rigour and discipline as they tackle operational transformations. They should provide frameworks, systems, and processes that continuously reinforce the right values – proactively engaging different audiences at more points on their journey, while confronting any challenges that distract or derail their culture from enabling the mission.

Recommendation 6: Collective ownership

Self-sustaining performance

Bilateral participation and collective accountability are far better at driving performance standards than command and control. As supply chains become more fragmented, it's vital to create a sense of shared ownership and belief across your business and encourage teams to take more active responsibility and mutual accountability.

Some organisations have appointed **cultural ambassadors** to cultivate and foster the right behaviours. Culture ambassadors don't have to be leaders, but they do need to be credible influencers who champion the right values and encourage a following, as well as holding people to account. Culture ambassadors can drive tailored programmes, organise specific events, and provide contextual guidance to 'localise' culture, while keeping it aligned to wider organisational values.

Once leaders have set the right course, they need to **get out of the way** as much as possible. Leaders have to trust capable talent of taking more responsibility. To trust in the culture and strategy and allow their teams to take more ownership. To build accountability by allowing others to lead. Organisations will not address their myriad challenges if all ideas, initiatives, and decisions have to flow through the same few individuals. Allow teams to own their performance.

Finally, **invite workforces to constantly shape the culture**. Cultures are living, breathing entities that evolve as businesses grow and market conditions change. Encourage new and existing employees to participate in how culture is nurtured, giving them a meaningful voice in shaping values and behaviours. Set up cross-company workshops to redesign employment experiences from recruitment through to alumni engagement programmes. Encourage employees to develop their own personalised culture adverts or incentivise teams to celebrate and recognise each other's victories and contributions, rather than relying on senior leadership.

Strengthen connections

Unlock collaboration, enabling teams to quickly react to change, respond to challenges, or create the offerings that customers want. **Leaders should act as cultural connectors**, spotting opportunities to unite key human capital from different parts of the organisation and creating an environment that enables constructive conversations.

Incentivise employees to network within the business, collaborating with colleagues outside their immediate teams while leveraging internal thought communities (see *Chapter 7: Positioning for Success*). Publish details of new workstreams and initiatives on your intranet, then invite input from across the business. Encourage internal teams to connect with their external suppliers and partners in an informal setting to share their interests with each other and create meaningful, work-related conversations.

Endorse and empower sharing, pooling relevant knowledge and increasing accessibility to anyone who may legitimately require it. Invest in an online portal where individuals can share industry intelligence, ask for support and opinions, and crowdsource solutions. Encourage broad involvement – helping teams and individuals to be constructively engaged and giving them a voice and platform to share.

> Platforms such as Rungway provide anonymous mentoring services at scale, and services such as Slack provide a range of collaboration tools and services to enable focused exchanges.

Leaders play an essential role listening and responding to queries, improving cross-functional connections, and encouraging honest and constructive feedback.

Inspire commitment and re-earn trust

Successful cultures are re-earned every day, resonating in every exchange between every part of the workforce. Culture should engender genuine trust and belief between employees, independent workers, and partners before it can do the same with clients, customers, and candidates. Performance improves when workforces are trusted to develop new ideas and solve their own problems.

Start by **trusting people with insights into the bigger picture**. Proactively publish executive perspectives that help them understand strategic objectives, supported by non-sensitive financial information. Openly share all relevant news and information – both positive and negative – to give the workforce a wider perspective. Publish metrics that demonstrate genuine progress (or the lack of it) on key strategic initiatives and projects, while sharing data on key internal metrics such as diversity or the gender pay gap.

Next, leaders should **give their teams more control**. Delegate low-risk projects, while allowing employees to work on the initiatives that they enjoy. Encourage employees to choose the kind of work they like to do, giving them an opportunity to shine. Reduce unnecessary rules and regulations, trusting your people to use the tools, systems, and processes that help them get the job done. Don't impose conformity, but instead liberate performance. Allow workers to use social media to communicate internally and externally, sharing an authentic view of your organisation.

Finally, **lead by example**. Senior leaders should share more about themselves and follow through on their commitments, only making promises about things that can be done. Don't ignore failures or mistakes; instead, acknowledge the problem and look for ways to fix it, showing fairness and consistency between and within teams. However, if there are individuals who, despite your best efforts to guide them, still display the wrong behaviours, leaders must act decisively to send the right message across the business.

Summary: Collective ownership

Micromanaging every detail of how people should behave is demoralising, inefficient, and impossible. Instead, create a sense of collective ownership, nurturing an environment where everyone is unified by a common set of values and beliefs while remaining free to be innovative and candid. Cultivate an atmosphere that self-reinforces positive behaviours and continually strives for better outcomes. Unlock collaboration to connect distributed teams so they can operate with speed and agility.

Culture

IMPACT OF FORCES

I4. Culture has become an essential leadership tool	*I5.* Engagement is harder to win and easier to lose	*I6.* Dependent on increasingly distributed and diverse workforce
Key driver of competitive advantage • Closer to all stakeholders • Critical to customer loyalty • Essential to innovation	**Cultural authenticity is increasingly important** • Shared, not replaced purpose and values • Cannot be bought • Greater emphasis on honesty and transparency	**Non-permanent workforce increasingly important** • Greater role in performance and productivity • Vital source of information and innovation • Growing source of risk
Underpins speed, consistency, and risk management • Key to speed and agility • Unified and consistent customer experiences • Balanced risk-taking	**Constantly and consistently reflected** • Demonstrate purpose, values, and behaviours • Every stage of the talent lifecycle • Professional and respectful to *everyone*	**Cultural consistency harder to maintain** • More culturally dynamic and diverse • Less opportunity to deepen cultural alignment • Established cultural practices less effective
Diminishing effectiveness of traditional performance management • Annualised performance review insufficient • Deferred career fulfilment less attractive • Short-term financial incentives less effective	**Culture much more visible** • Company and manager ratings • Insights from independent peer-review platforms • Inconsistencies much more exposed	

RECOMMENDATIONS ➤ ACTIVATE

ACTIVATE

R4. Build intrinsic strength	*R5.* Intentional culture	*R6.* Empower collective ownership
Distil authentic identity • Invest in a culture audit • Scaled-to-fit capacity, demand, and timescales • Honestly and openly review the results	**Constant, clear, prescriptive** • Provide the next layer of guidance • Prioritise standards • Values and guidance regularly communicated	**Self-sustaining performance** • Cultural ambassadors • Get out of the way • Invite workforces to constantly shape your culture
Recalibrated culture • Define and embrace authentic, natural values • Augment with essential attributes needed for the digital age • Align collective values to your purpose	**Proactive communication** • Encourage continuous transparency • Show, rather than tell • Incentivise workforce to create and share their own authentic experiences	**Strengthen connections** • Leaders act as cultural connectors • Incentivise networking • Endorse and empower sharing
Genuine, long-term investment • CEOs and Executives relaunch recalibrated culture • Set and measure behaviour goals • Budget for ongoing cultural investments	**Uncork culture** • Integrated and complementary talent experiences • Upgrade people infrastructure to support updated values • Retrain all leaders	**Inspire commitment and re-earn trust** • Provide insights into the bigger picture • Give teams more control • Lead by example

CHAPTER 6

Structure and Leadership

There are two types of organisational structure. Physical structures, which look at the relationships between tangible elements such as buildings and places where work is conducted, and social structures, which refer to relationships between people, positions, and organisational units. Organisational structure is a system that predominantly addresses social structures, defines hierarchy, and determines how "roles, power and responsibility are assigned, controlled and coordinated and how information flows between different levels of management".[1]

Organisational leadership typically provides objectives, operational oversight, inspiration, and various administrative services to a business. Effective leadership can help prioritise objectives for employees, independent workers, and partners, providing guidance in achieving the overall corporate vision.[2] Together, structure and leadership define how work is organised and controlled to achieve objectives – and how workflows, procedures, systems, and management interact.

Organisational design (OD) helps businesses to identify the workflows and structures that don't operate as intended, then update them to better deliver objectives within the current business reality. Good OD can accelerate the speed at which businesses operate, providing a clear line of sight between activity and results, and increasing organisational agility, innovation, engagement, and performance. Poor OD can result in a "bewildering morass of contradictions: confusion within roles, a lack of co-ordination among functions, failure to share ideas, and slow decision-making bringing managers unnecessary complexity, stress, and conflict".[3]

Why should leaders care?

Structure and leadership play a much more important role in the digital age. Organisations have to work faster, change direction more regularly, and deploy constantly changing skills to answer relentlessly shifting customer demand. Leaders must extract greater value from their workforces over shorter timescales to exploit smaller windows of opportunity. They have to better allocate organisational risks to compete with completely different business models. They must inspire and engage human capital with different and dynamic aspirations. Much more than just the definition of hierarchy, roles, and responsibilities – structure and leadership are fundamental to growth and wealth creation.

Impact of the forces

In today's business world, pressure on leaders is mounting as they struggle to balance evolving demands with a more autonomous, distributed, and diverse workforce – one that they also have less control over. Co-location and large, owned workforces no longer offer the same advantages as they once did. In addition, traditional organisational structures, detailed process flows, and legacy approaches cannot operate at the speed, accuracy, and quality required in the digital age.

Impact 7: Established organisational certainties are undermined

The advantages of size are diminishing

Bigger no longer means better. Traditionally, larger companies had a clear advantage, as economic certainty (powered by liberal capitalism) enabled them to take long-term views on risk. They could vertically integrate their organisations to achieve fantastic economies of scale. However, as we saw in Part 1, that certainty has been disrupted. Now, organisations can scale, accelerate, and expand their offering – all without having to significantly invest in a proportional increase in their operating infrastructure. This has reduced the commercial advantage that large, vertically integrated organisations once had over their smaller rivals.

New economic models (as seen in *Chapter 1: Political, Economic, and Commercial Instability*) are reducing organisations' dependency on large permanent workforces. Huge, owned workforces not only mean significant capital expenditure, but also extensive operational costs from day-to-day administration, extra layers of management, pensions, healthcare, and bonus plans.

On the other hand, increasingly efficient and effective partner models enable organisations to access external experts without adding to the headcount. Third parties don't need additional physical infrastructure, carry the same fixed operating costs, or require the same layers of management as their permanent contemporaries. Productivity and quality can be improved without a corresponding increase in fixed costs.

In addition, AI and automation are reducing the amount of human capital required to deliver products and services. As smart factories evolve, fewer highly skilled workers are replacing large numbers of lower-skilled human capital. Technology is also enabling many traditional office-based roles to be automated, reducing the requirement to house large, permanent workforces under one roof.

> The accountancy and legal professions are already augmented by robotic process automation and the financial services industry is supported by algorithms that deliver faster, more efficient analysis and assessment.

Finally, evidence is mounting that commercial success is no longer dependent on scale. While size can provide powerful competitive benefits, companies that create the most value no longer rely on being the biggest.

> According to a Bain & Co. report, 40% of all economic leaders are not the largest business in their sector. They reference Germany's Continental Tires, which is three times more profitable than Japan's Bridgestone, despite being much smaller.[4]

The advantages of physical centralisation are declining

Traditionally, physical centralisation enabled businesses to improve productivity through closer management of human activity. Opportunities for internal communication and collaboration were enhanced, as was control of everyday tasks, adherence to processes, and tighter management of data security. Some of these advantages remain true, with many organisations preferring to aggregate their workforces in single-site core locations. However, for many companies, the benefits of co-location are waning.

Firstly, the high fixed costs of large real estate increases operational risk. Organisations with large physical footprints (especially in centralised locations to make them accessible to the largest talent pools) carry significantly inflated operational costs tied into higher rents over inflexible timescales. Unless businesses are so cash-rich that these costs are inconsequential, large real estate can significantly impact on operational cash flow, restricting their ability to capitalise on fast-moving opportunities.

Secondly, the need for physically localised infrastructure is reducing. Customer data, experiences, and transactions increasingly take place in the cloud. Technology is removing the constraints of location from customer interactions. Supply chain interfaces and commercial coordination are becoming more and more virtualised, either with horizontally aligned partners or vertically aligned colleagues. Business processes and procedures can be monitored and managed from anywhere – and leaders can connect and engage their teams effectively using collaboration software.

Finally, the requirement for human capital to be physically present can restrict access to critical talent. As markets move faster and work decouples from location, competitive advantage comes from accessing and deploying the best talent *regardless* of their location. Organisations that require workers to physically co-locate limit the size of their talent pools. The best talent may not want or be able to commute or permanently relocate. And with access to more opportunities, many won't have to. As people pursue multi-stage lifestyles, more workers will choose employers that support location flexibility, enabling them to balance their careers with their other commitments.

The talent ownership model is being challenged

As with real estate, large permanent headcounts mean large fixed operational costs, which in turn restrict commercial agility. At the same time, new economic conditions make it easier, cheaper, and more productive to outsource elements of a business. Likewise, efficient partnering reduces the demand for multiple hierarchical layers, increasing speed of thought and action. In addition, new external talent platforms mean that higher-value skills can be deployed in more cost-effective ways. All of this is challenging the traditional concept of 'owning' the workforce.

On-demand external providers are now better positioned to deliver superior products and services faster with less risk. Organisations require rapid access to unpredictable skills to capitalise on profitable opportunities, quickly shutting down initiatives that are no longer effective or in demand. Increased access to specialists on demand enables organisations to deploy talent to projects instead of roles, where they only work for the time they are needed to complete specific objectives. As specialists, they develop deeper knowledge and are more exposed to the latest sector developments, while their remuneration can be directly indexed to performance.

Impact summary: Changing organisational certainties

Companies are rethinking the size, shape, and physical distribution of their organisational structures. The increasing virtualisation of the workforce is reducing organisations' dependency on centralising human capital under one roof. Shifting economic models and fluctuations in underlying operating costs are increasing the risks associated with 'owning' real estate and headcount.

Impact 8: Move faster, adapt quicker, and deliver different outcomes

The reduced effectiveness of rigid workflows and hierarchies

Today, production lifecycles are shorter and markets are evolving faster. This means that workflows, systems, processes, and tools must constantly adapt to keep pace with demand. Braver decisions have to be made faster to exploit gaps or preserve market share. Unfortunately, rigid structures and workflows that prioritise process compliance, or defer to rank, struggle to keep up with flatter, more autonomous approaches.

Speed of delivery is replacing compliance as a driver of competitive advantage. Previously, organisational structures were built to deliver incremental efficiencies. They had large, complicated hierarchies and multiple processes to ensure workflow alignment and delivery control. However, fast markets and faster competitors mean it's more important to react quickly, rather than conform to rigid structures and hierarchies.

> Toyota learned this to their detriment in 2010, when they were forced to recall 8 million vehicles due to a fault with unintended acceleration. Their hierarchical structure and compliant culture prevented bad news from being passed up the chain quickly, allowing a small safety problem to snowball into a corporate catastrophe.[5]

For firms today, adaptability is business-critical. The more formalised layers and leaders a company has, the less agile it becomes. Decisions that have to filter through more levels not only travel slower, but are also at increased risk of misinterpretation and confusion over ownership. Ultimately, the more layers in a hierarchy, the further away decision-makers are from their customers. As such, many companies are flattening their structures or relaxing their hierarchies to mitigate this risk.

> In 2015, Alcoa announced that it was splitting into an upstream and downstream business to compete more effectively in two separate marketplaces.[6] 3M is strongly committed to decentralisation to encourage innovation, with close to 100 profit centres. Meanwhile, Ikea are using flatter hierarchies within its stores to build stronger employee engagement and ownership.[7]

Quality outcomes, not quantity outputs

Today's value chains are shifting away from a focus on production efficiency. Successful structures and workflows are prioritising experience over service, removing the barriers for workers to develop new solutions. They are also encouraging the entire workforce, including outsourced providers, to deliver superior customer interactions over cost savings or task optimisation.

Service is now a prerequisite for customers and no longer delivers competitive advantage on its own. As consumers become increasingly discerning and have access to more suppliers, many organisations are reconfiguring their workflows and processes to deliver positive experiences throughout the customer lifecycle.

> Zappos employees are targeted to build personal connections to deepen customer relationships. Netflix creates hyper-personalised recommendations based on customer data to help users find the content they want to see.[8]

Organisations now depend on a constant supply of innovation to deliver the enhancements that consumers value the most. Structures and workflows have to empower their workforces not only to come up with new ideas, but to rapidly escalate, test, and apply them. Incremental improvements to existing tasks struggle to deliver against elevated demand, while an emphasis on process compliance suppresses creativity and employee motivation.

Finally, the increased demand for quality and consistency throughout the customer lifecycle disrupts outsourcing approaches that prioritise the reduction of operational costs. Outsourcing based on price can significantly undermine the customer experience.

Organisations that pass off critical parts of their supply chain to partners that are incentivised to do it at the lowest price significantly increase the risk of damaging their reputation. Many US and UK banks offshored their customer-service operations to India based on cost, only to repatriate many of those operations due to negative customer feedback.

Dynamic accuracy is essential

Organisations have narrower windows of opportunity to achieve their goals, plus more distractions and less time to correct if they go off course. In this climate, mistakes are amplified, organisational friction increases, and chances are quickly lost. This means that organisations must now constantly monitor, align, and adjust their processes and workflows to ensure their teams remain continually focused on the highest-value activities.

For example, the risk of 'unintentionality' is dramatically increased in the digital age. Unintentionality*, as defined by organisational design experts Morven Jones, is the naturally occurring, almost inevitable irrationality or bias that sits alongside the rational, hard-headed decisions that organisations make. Every leader and every leadership team has an existing bias in their interpretation of their organisation's purpose, values, and strategy.

Many leaders, without being consciously aware, occasionally behave unintentionally as a result of this bias – creating a divergence between the intended objectives of the business strategy and the actions that the business actually takes. Unintentionality can happen anywhere and at any scale, such as adopting misleading metrics to measure productivity, encouraging inappropriate behaviours to drive profitability, or outsourcing based on incorrectly defined goals. In this age, minor misunderstandings and mistakes quickly accumulate into major diversions that pull businesses away from their intended objectives.

Workflows and processes are now dynamically adapting to more fluid operational goals. Constant experimentation has become necessary to facilitate faster adaptation to real-world scenarios. Many organisations are developing iterative process improvements to ensure their teams remain focused on the highest-value activity. Indeed, the agile software development methodology favoured by numerous technology firms has been co-opted by many management teams who have learned that "continuing the management practices and structures of the lumbering industrial giants of the 20th century won't cut the mustard".[9]

Competitive advantage increasingly comes from constantly incorporating real-time learnings into workflows and processes.

In his book *Black Box Thinking* (John Murray, 2016), Matthew Syed wrote about success and failure using the analogy of aircraft black boxes, where previous data gathered provides information from all aircraft failures – and that has made planes the safest form of travel. In short, embracing failure, learning lessons, and adapting quickly delivers ongoing improvements.

As organisations race to keep up with constantly changing demand, many enterprises are now regularly and quickly modifying their workflows based on customer feedback and real-time experiences to give themselves an edge.

* The distinction and implications of intentionality and unintentionality are copyright of Morven Jones, as is how to include this distinction into organisation design theory and schematics

Impact summary: Different outcomes

Structures and hierarchies are evolving to capitalise on narrowing windows of opportunity. Activities have to be completed quickly and accurately, adapting to faster-changing circumstances while delivering different outcomes. Workflows are continually updating to ensure that teams remain focused on the highest-value actions.

Impact 9: More pressure on leaders at all levels

Expected to do more

Leaders are expected to deliver better results, faster, and in increasingly competitive environments. Instead of driving incremental efficiencies, leaders need to refocus their teams on higher-value customer experiences, creating new offerings that excite and delight consumers. This requires sifting through expanding volumes of information, extrapolating more tangible insights, and making better decisions faster. They also have to inspire more distributed teams to make the right decisions independently.

Nowadays, leaders are expected to deliver meaningful innovation more frequently. Competitive advantage comes from fresh ideas that answer the new questions posed by changing market conditions. Consumer engagement and loyalty are dependent on continually creating new experiences and offerings that customers value.

To improve their chances of creating the right solutions, it's increasingly critical for leaders to get closer to their customers to understand what they want, both now and in the future. They need to create the right conditions for their teams to come up with ideas, while getting their organisation to change fast enough to extract value in compressed timeframes.

Responsibility lies with leaders to constantly break down the growing barriers to performance. Greater volumes of information increase the organisational distractions that their teams face, and constantly changing competitive landscapes divert their teams' attention. Growing economic uncertainty can undermine their teams' confidence – in turn pushing responsibility and decisions back up the hierarchy, creating bottlenecks. Additionally, the destabilising of commercial models reinforces existing silos and amplifies the behaviours that prevent teams from collaborating effectively, increasing organisational friction.

Finally, leaders have to unify more distributed, diverse, and disparate workforces. More fragmented teams have more fragmented motivations, making them harder to engage, manage, and blend together into a coherent and functioning unit. Leaders have to effectively blend more remote workers from more diverse backgrounds, and from more generations, in more locations, working more flexibly.

A growing proportion of the workforce is independent, hired onto projects instead of roles, increasing the complexity of cultural alignment. And as more parts of the supply chain are passed off to third-party partners, leaders have to focus more on strategic consistency and continuity.

Top-down leadership is less effective

Top down, one-way leadership styles, such as command and control, are struggling to deliver the quality of outcomes demanded at the speed required. Predicated on the understanding that those higher up the hierarchy always know better than those lower down, top-down leadership ensures that decisions flow in only one direction – with more junior members of the hierarchy expected to execute instructions without complaint. However, these approaches undermine the trust and mutual respect that is vital for agile, innovative organisations, restricting an organisation's ability to adapt to changing realities.

Top-down hierarchies can significantly restrict agility at a time when businesses need it the most. They impede information-sharing, collaboration, and problem-solving, inhibiting businesses from overcoming the many challenges they face.

> In his book *Outliers* (Penguin, 2009), Malcolm Gladwell suggested that the hierarchical leadership of Korean Air was allowing preventable accidents to happen. He quoted the accident rate between 1988 and 1998 as being 17 times higher than a comparable carrier. While there were multiple contributing factors, Gladwell identified the organisation's hierarchy as the key issue. Passengers were dying because junior crew weren't allowed to question senior crew, even when there was compelling information to support them.

Unsurprisingly, top-down approaches disengage an evolving workforce with changing employment aspirations. As with culture, engagement now plays a much greater role in delivering performance and competitive advantage. However, productivity falls when human capital is treated like a disposable asset. Detailed instructions and tight supervision undermine mutual trust and respect, especially when it comes from a manager that may not be as close to the coalface. Performance suffers when staff do not experience a shared sense of purpose and values with their leaders and managers.

Finally, top-down leadership can restrict innovation. Innovation suffers when junior employees or third-party providers aren't given the freedom to come up with new ideas, let alone pass them back up the chain. Workforces find it difficult to create better customer experiences when their leaders don't give them ownership of problems and solutions – or fail to actively support and empower them to contribute. Talent stops coming up with new solutions when leaders take credit for successes up the chain of command or pass accountability for failures down the hierarchy.

Impact summary: Leadership pressure

It's getting harder for leaders to lead. Managers at all levels are required to deliver more, improve innovation, get closer to customers, and engage more sceptical, distributed, and autonomous workforces. As a result, many established leadership approaches are struggling to deliver results.

Optimising in the digital age

Despite the forces of change and resulting impacts, many organisations stick to the same structures, workflows, processes, and systems of the past. They predominantly 'own' their workforces, controlling activity in centralised real estate. They keep the same rigid and detailed workflows, enforcing process compliance through extensive rules and regulations, and maintain the same top-down management approaches.

However, these approaches are starting to limit productivity, profitability, and performance. Instead, organisations have to redesign their structures and workflows to deliver *intended results*, not reactive tasks. Leaders need to unclog organisational configurations and hierarchy, evolving the shape and size of their business to reduce organisational drag, costs, and liabilities. They need to liberate their leaders to inspire performance, not control actions.

Recommendation 7: Redesign for dynamic results

Redesign backwards

According to organisational design (OD) experts Jane Reay Jones and Arthur Jones of Morven Jones, the critical first step for an enterprise when designing its organisational structures is to be clear on what business it is and the commercial environment it operates in. Too narrow a focus and the organisational structure will not deliver the intended results, no matter how well it organises itself. Too broad and it will overstretch itself by going where it lacks knowledge and competence, diluting its ability to deliver in business areas where it is adept.

Using your clarified purpose (recommended in *Chapter 4: The Plan*), accurately

define what is required of your organisation now and in the future. Organisations cannot design the right structure until they understand exactly what their business needs to do today and what it will need to do tomorrow. Additionally, use your multiple sources of competitive intelligence to develop an accurate assessment of your current operating environment. Collectively, this information defines your business situation.

Next, **compare your business situation to your current results**. How well does your organisation deliver The Plan in the current operating environment? How well are customer needs met, is the organisation achieving its financial objectives, are you defending against competitive threats, how well does the business cope with localised social, political, or legal expectations etc? This gap analysis identifies which parts of your structure are delivering intended results and which parts require attention.

Use the same process to **define the core workflows and processes** that deliver current and future organisational goals – as well as the **critical structural components** that enable their delivery. Assess the value added at each layer of hierarchy to help understand your essential leadership requirements. Only by understanding the current and future results that workflows and processes must deliver can business effectively redesign their organisational structures.

Distil core workflows into the key steps that are critical to success, and establish which parts of the supply chain need to remain in-house, and which can be done by external partners. Only by understanding the current and future results that workflows and processes must deliver can business effectively redesign their organisational structures.

Upgrade the value chain

Next, **evaluate the capability, competence and capacity** of each team within your value chain. Start by mapping the value chain to understand who does what in delivering products and services to customers and clients, pinpointing natural strengths and obvious weaknesses. Identify which teams will deliver the most critical workflows and forecast how well they deliver them.

Next, **measure the difference** between your workforce's current capability and their ability to deliver intended results in your updated organisational design. Starting with the highest-value core workflows, define any gaps, then forecast the cost benefit to close them. For example, are there external providers who can deliver better quality more cost-effectively? Is upskilling more cost-effective than outsourcing? Is there technology available that could deliver more consistent results more cost-effectively over the long term? What is the impact on fixed and variable costs within the supply chain by bringing outsourced roles back in-house?

Once you have completed this evaluation, set up an internal **cross-functional programme to methodically close the gaps**. Develop relationships with alternate suppliers, consider new talent supply models, and explore new training options to fully understand the choices and costs.

While investing in internal teams can often close the gap quickest and at the lowest risk and cost, new technology and economic models offer progressively viable replacements. Start small and test solutions with ring-fenced parts of the business, learning how to apply changes and mitigate risks (we investigate commercial experimentation in more depth in *Chapter 8: Operational Excellence*).

Design for dynamic equilibrium

Structures and workflows must be able to deliver tomorrow as well as today, adapting to change as soon as external forces demand it. Processes and systems that have agility 'baked in' are able to change direction quickly to support the continued success of the business. Effective communication across interconnected teams enables relevant human capital to effectively coordinate activity, adjusting work practices to maintain focus on core objectives.

To do this, **embed 'fail fast' thinking** within all of your workflows. Processes ought to reward innovation, not punish non-compliance.

> According to Adam Grant, creator of the +Acumen Master Class, failure shouldn't be embraced, but it should be normalised.[10]

Stop workflows emphasising perfection and caution and start emphasising sharing and continuous feedback. Testing multiple iterations is a core feature of design thinking – workflows and processes must not only enable experimentation but *encourage* it.

Understanding the **evolving demands of your customers** in real time helps the workflows and processes that deliver them to evolve. Link key teams to customer feedback loops (described in the next chapter), ensuring they are continuously updated. To develop a single, true, and consistent understanding of the customer, limit the number of these loops, and feed insights back into a coordinated, organisation-wide customer experience programme.

Support this approach with **open communication channels** that ensure everyone shares relevant information. All teams, internal and external, need to have a thorough understanding of what each other is doing and why they are doing it. However, it's vital to develop only the essential channels that ensure information can flow, while guarding against overwhelming people with too much data. This requires some basic guidelines on what qualifies as being 'worth sharing'.

In addition, leverage existing communication platforms to ensure that relevant teams are not only connected but 'on the same page'. Set up project communities and invite impacted representatives from across the business. Eliminate information bottlenecks such as email cascades so access to information is not limited by hierarchy. Encourage feedback and communication across the entire supply chain, regularly connecting decision-makers with each other to improve functional coordination.

Recommendation summary: Redesign for dynamic results

To get the right OD for your business, start with the results you are trying to achieve and work backwards – redesigning and realigning the structures, systems, and processes that deliver your clarified purpose. Upgrade your value chain, selecting the internal and external providers that can cost-effectively deliver the highest-quality results. Any business can remain dynamically relevant, no matter what the market conditions – if they build adaptability into their workflows while improving the connections between different parts of the workforce.

Recommendation 8: Reduce organisational drag

Identify and adjust for unintentionality

Leaders and decision-makers have to guard against the activities that unintentionally slow down or divert effort away from the strategy. Implementing a structural reorganisation without a fundamental review of the beliefs and biases within the organisation (as many change efforts do) is unlikely to produce any sustainable improvements in the results the business delivers. Organisations end up addressing the *symptoms* of organisational drag, not the *causes*, which can in fact lead to more distractions, confusion, and poorer business results.

For example, a desire to provide more career promotion opportunities to engage talent can result in increased layers in an organisation. Extra layers lead to fragmentation of work, which is then not executed at the appropriate level or with the appropriate skillsets. Entire teams end up operating at the wrong grade, leading to disengagement and underperformance.

First, **make leadership beliefs and biases transparent**. Pay attention to verbatim comments from employee surveys or feedback loops. Make skip-level conversations (when employees meet directly with their manager's manager) part of your regular business activities. Facilitate open, meaningful, and 'safe' conversations with human capital to provide insights into what is really rewarded, what information is shared or not, what decisions are made and by whom, and how work really gets done.

Routinely **compile evidence of 'ghost strategies'**, where leader actions and directions divert or distract teams away from your actual strategy. Measure the direct and indirect impact of these approaches, paying particular attention to the effects outside the immediate team or function. Comparing your unintentional strategy with your intended one provides detailed, empirical evidence and insights to help you identify the biases and beliefs that slow your business down.

Regularly address unintentionality. Share headline data openly with your leadership teams to highlight how unintentionality undermines the intended strategy. Encourage your leaders to do the same with their teams, encouraging them to be constantly vigilant. This sets the scene for a shift in leadership style, and even the hierarchy required to manage the business effectively.

Unclog structures and empower relationships

Structures should empower autonomy, create speed, ensure focus, and enable agility – driving progress and innovation from the ground up. Maintaining positive organisational relationships is essential to improving trust and shared beliefs that empower consistency and increased commitment to purpose. Optimising the size and shape of interdependent units helps organisations to adapt quicker, perform better, and manage operational risk more effectively.

Try **organising teams around strategic projects** instead of functions. Cross-functional project teams that focus on key strategic objectives such as 'customer engagement' or 'revenue growth' better align work activities to strategic results. They are less distracted by the departmental rules and regulations associated with functional teams. They also more clearly define how individual and team efforts contribute to organisational goals, making it easier to identify and blend in the required external skills and experience.

Experiment with the size of operating units. Large groups require more hierarchy, rules, and regulation to command loyalty and cohesion. In smaller groups, it's possible to achieve trust and belief informally, with unruly behaviour controlled on the basis of personal loyalties and peer-to-peer contacts.

British anthropologist Robin Dunbar suggested the optimal team size is 150-200, above which "there is a cognitive limit to the number of individuals with whom any one person can maintain stable relationships, and this limits group size".[11]

Clearly, there is a balance to strike between creating smaller, nimbler teams and atomising complexity. However, developing organisational units within this threshold may help improve team unity, break down the barriers to collaboration, and empower teams to deliver more with less leadership input.

Finally, **review all the layers of hierarchy** within the organisation and look at ways to strip back any unnecessary levels that stifle performance and innovation – leaving only the layers that are crucial to delivering the intended strategy. This encourages and engages critical frontline talent to innovate, iteratively improving and spreading their ideas through faster feedback loops. It also reduces the operational drag of an unintended culture that is magnified through multiple layers. Carefully consider which layers are removed. For example, removing the most expensive layer of the hierarchy doesn't necessarily deliver cost savings.

Less is more

As structures become unclogged, review the guidelines that govern the execution of workflows to make sure they are simple, essential, and efficient. Move away from the onerous regulations that controlled yesterday's tasks towards empowered guidance that delivers tomorrow's results. Work towards an approach where anyone can lead if they are given clear principles and parameters to make decisions.

The **workflows have to be simple and accurate**. While workflows themselves streamline repeatable business actions, to be effective they must be easy to apply for anyone who interacts with them. As workforces diversify and the volume of people coming in and out of businesses increases, simplicity and ease of application are essential.

Large, complicated, multi-step process maps might help to mitigate operational risks, but if they are too convoluted and complicated to be easily applied, the risk of divergence from strategy far outweighs the benefits of compliance. Make workflows short and simple, only including the critical steps that deliver essential strategic outcomes. Boil processes down to their essence to improve accuracy of application and enable speed.

Next, organisations should consider which **policies, rules, and regulations are essential to the delivery of their intended strategy**. Modern workforces quickly disengage from complicated rules and regulations that require them to do things in a certain way at a certain time, to follow orders, or do as they're told. Instead, try relaxing the rules that don't deliver a clear, demonstrable advantage. Businesses that allow their teams to dictate the method and processes to achieve clearly defined goals have more engaged and productive workforces.

Finally, **consider principles instead of rule-based business frameworks**. Principle-based frameworks enable operational flexibility and empowerment while maintaining focus on strategic goals. Essential policies, rules, and regulations can exist within a principle-based framework, enabling speed while ensuring that behaviours remain in line with an organisation's purpose and values. A shift away from enforcing process compliance and organisational standardisation releases existing line managers to focus on higher-value activities and can reduce the requirement for supervisory layers.

Recommendation summary: Reduce drag

Target unintentional activities, proactively holding up the mirror to beliefs and biases that divert effort away from the strategy. Address the legacy structures, rules, and behaviours that may inadvertently restrict your refreshed and dynamic workflows from adding value. Focus on entrenched organisational configurations that unconsciously slow down critical processes and decision-making. Improve efficiency and effectiveness by distilling workflows, processes, and rules to their essence, making them easier and more likely to be followed.

Recommendation 9: Lead instead of manage

Redefine leadership

Clarify what leadership means in your organisation, starting with the difference between leaders and managers. Leaders inspire; managers control. Leaders ask; managers tell. Leaders encourage questions; managers encourage compliance. Redefining the role of leadership across the organisation is essential to realise the power of culture.

Define the different types of leadership your organisation needs to succeed. Too often, senior executives get caught up in the day-to-day workings of the business, preventing them from working on the strategic objectives that drive long-term profitability. Too often, junior leaders prioritise urgent over important, unintentionally changing the activities of their teams to work on lower-value initiatives. Too often, both levels resort to command and control to deliver tasks.

Senior leaders are there to enable the vision, paint the big picture, and positively frame necessary change. They are not there to optimise the present, but rather to extract underlying potential, setting out what needs to happen to achieve strategic objectives. They should regularly remove themselves from the environment to clear their head of the daily noise of business and stop getting sucked into operational challenges. They should spend time with other senior leaders outside of normal business demands to broaden their perspectives and break down silos, and make time to truly understand their customers.

Junior leaders lead the execution. Striving to remove operational barriers to their teams' performance, junior leaders inspire innovation while keeping everyone focused on the big picture. They reinforce the connection between each individual's purpose and the organisation's purpose and reduce the risk of operational distractions. They showcase the organisation's values every day, challenging negative behaviours while working hard to unify all parts of the organisation's distributed workforce.

Empower self-leadership and cooperation

There is too much for leaders to do all by themselves, especially when responsibility is pushed back up the chain by teams and individuals uncertain about what to do. Instead, encourage your teams to take more responsibility, empowering them to think and act beyond the confines of job descriptions or departmental silos.

Decentralise decision-making to help them become more autonomous. Some organisations, such as Google and Ernst & Young, are experimenting with 'holacracy', a way of structuring and running an organisation that replaces conventional management hierarchies. Instead of operating top-down, power is distributed throughout the organisation, giving individuals and teams more freedom to self-manage, while staying aligned to the organisation's purpose. Holacracy has a written constitution that replaces many of the essential elements traditionally delivered by managers. An "explicit and lightweight ruleset sets clear expectations and makes the decision-making authority transparent at every level", underwriting cooperation, ownership, clarity, and alignment.[11]

Alternatively, try **delegating to the lowest level of competence** to strip out unnecessary supervisory positions. If the lowest levels within the organisation have all the right information and are empowered, they can make great decisions without leaders needing to approve, ratify, or control. This not only liberates leaders to focus on the bigger picture, but also reduces the number of layers that an organisation requires. In turn, this speeds up decision-making and improves engagement.

Finally, experiment **with the 'player-coach' model**. Defined as individual contributors managing the work of others, this is not about one person performing two roles, but about empowering star players to transfer their brilliance to those around them. Enabling and rewarding the strongest individuals to inspire others – and share their passion, insights, and understanding – is a powerful tool to get workers to take more responsibility.

Henry Ford, Thomas Edison, and Steve Jobs all successfully performed player-coach roles where their individual brilliance and passion for their work connected their teams to the mission, collaboratively propelling teams forward.[12]

Become conductors

A part of every leader's role is to be a *conductor*, ensuring that the flow of information powers thought, innovation, and collaboration. While everyone in a business should share relevant information with those around them, senior leaders play an enhanced role, proactively capturing and communicating key customer insights while simultaneously deepening connections and strengthening relationships across the supply chain.

Top-down leadership styles tend to limit a leader's understanding of the day-to-day reality of their customer's experience. Information from the front line doesn't flow back up the structure, limiting leaders' access the relevant insights they need to make good decisions. Instead, **senior leaders must connect directly with customers** to understand the daily reality of their experience. Notwithstanding the distributed autonomy suggested in *Chapter 4: The Plan*, senior leaders within your organisation should regularly spend time on site with their clients or consumer focus groups, working with other senior leaders to develop one true view of the customer and ensuring that a unified definition is shared with the rest of the business.

Urge all leaders to understand the parts of their business outside their immediate theatre of operation and become **cross-functional conductors**. Incentivise them to break down the traditional silos that have prevented collaboration by spending time 'in their colleagues' shoes', understanding their challenges and opportunities and proactively communicating this back to their teams. Teams who have mutual respect and understanding collaborate more effectively and invest discretionary time and effort to solve problems quicker.

Finally, leaders are **conductors for their external partners**. As a proportion of work is increasingly delivered by independent workers and external providers, leaders play a critical role in strengthening these relationships, aligning and engaging external teams and individuals to deliver the best results for their customers. Leaders should tie partner performance metrics and rewards to the achievement of strategic results, not tactical tasks. They should also reinforce the importance of their own company values and behaviours in all interactions. In addition, developing closer ties with key partners helps them to tap into potentially rich sources of information and innovation, sharing any insights back to their teams.

Recommendation summary: Lead, don't manage

Leadership is about inspiring human capital to solve problems themselves, rather than commanding and controlling their every action. Teams must be empowered and inspired to develop game-changing innovations, rather than being cajoled into delivering incremental efficiencies. Great talent should be quickly connected to the right opportunity to extract maximum value, rather than being locked into rigid functional hierarchies. Leaders must learn how to lead, instead of manage, to liberate their teams to deliver commercial results, and to empower their entire supply chain to deliver the consistent, compelling experiences that customers expect.

Structure and Leadership

IMPACT OF FORCES

I7. *Organisational certainties undermined*	**I8.** *Move faster, adapt quicker, and deliver different outcomes*	**I9.** *More pressure on leaders at all levels*
Advantages of size diminishing • Bigger no longer means better • AI and automation reduce amount of human capital • Success not dependent on scale	**Reduced effectiveness of rigid workflows and hierarchies** • Speed of delivery replaces compliance • Adaptability business-critical	**Expected to do more** • Deliver meaningful innovations more frequently • Constantly breakdown barriers to performance • Unify distributed, diverse, and disparate workforce
Advantages of physical centralisation declining • High fixed costs of large real estate increase risk • Reduced need for physical corporate infrastructure • Access to, and optimisation of, talent restricted	**Demand for quality outcomes not quantity outputs** • Service no longer enough • Deliver constant supply of innovation • Outsourcing on task and cost alone undermines reputation	**Top-down leadership less effective** • Top-down hierarchies restrict agility • Disengage evolving workforce • Restrict innovation and productivity
Talent ownership model challenged • External providers better at delivering ROI • External providers mean better products and faster services • Greater variety & range of external workforce solutions	**Dynamic accuracy essential** • Risk of 'unintentionality' increased • Workflows must adapt to more fluid goals • Real-time learnings must be incorporated quickly	

RECOMMENDATIONS — ACTIVATE →

R7. *Redesign for dynamic results*	**R8.** *Reduce organisational drag*	**R9.** *Lead instead of manage*
Redesign backwards • Define what is required now and in the future • Compare business situation to current results • Define core workflows and processes	**Identify and adjust for unintentionality** • Make leadership beliefs and biases transparent • Compile evidence of 'ghost strategies' • Regularly address unintentionality	**Redefine leadership** • Define types of leadership needed • Senior leaders enable the vision • Junior leaders lead the execution
Upgrade the value chain • Evaluate capability, competence and capacity of current supply • Measure gap between current capability and updated design • Cross-functional programme to close the gaps	**Unclog structures and empower relationships** • Organise around strategic projects not functions • Experiment with size of operating units • Review hierarchical layers	**Empower self-leadership and cooperation** • Decentralise decision-making • Delegate to lowest level of competence • Experiment with player-coach model
Design for dynamic equilibrium • Embed 'fail fast' thinking • Constantly track evolving customer demand • Open communication channels	**Less is more** • Simple and accurate workflows • Minimise policies, rules, and regulations • Principles-based framework	**Become conductors** • Customer conductors • Cross-functional conductors • External partner conductors

ACTIVATE

CHAPTER 7

Positioning for Success

Positioning is the activity of creating, communicating, and delivering offerings that have value for consumers. Positioning and extracting value are at the heart of the business model – moving beyond just the marketing department to include product management, operations, sales, and customer relations. To deliver a successful offering, businesses need to coordinate all of these functions to reach, resonate with, and motivate customers to realise a monetary reward.

This requires a proposition delivering an overarching promise of a product, service, or company to the marketplace. It defines the output of the business – encompassing a range of functional and emotional benefits that consumers get. It also highlights the advantages of using that product, service, or company over a competing solution. All of this requires a deep understanding of the target market and empathy for their evolving needs.

Any "marketing communication used to inform or persuade a target audience about the merits of a product, service, brand, or issue are referred to as 'promotion'. The aim of promotion is to increase awareness, create interest, generate sales, or create brand loyalty."[1] Promotion often focuses on a target audience and compels them to take action.

Finally, positioning requires delivery in a timely, expected fashion against what was promised. Delivery must be done in a manner that reflects customers' expectations – not only of the product, but also of the brand, the company, and its values.

Why should leaders care?

Good positioning reduces risk, improves margins, and creates compelling propositions that resonate with consumers. It differentiates organisations from their competitors and also addresses customers' specific problems. Positioning establishes how value is created, informing everything from the content of messages to the way that services are shaped and prices are structured.

Creating and conveying a value proposition helps customers to understand why they should care, engage, and buy. Effective promotion differentiates an authentic offering to the right consumers with a compelling call to action. Excellent delivery reinforces emotional connections – driving loyalty, repeat business, and ultimately creating a healthy, sustainable company.

Impact of the forces

Consumers now expect constant and rapid reinvention. The digital world is changing everything from the very products sold to their promotion and tactical delivery. Many products now exist only in digital form, and promotion is increasingly global, while selling and buying take place 24/7. Pricing is much more competitive as new economic models enable competitors to offer similar products at significantly lower costs and online marketplaces allow direct sellers to set their own rates. The internet empowers promotion far more cheaply than a physical shop window, print advertising, or TV. In addition, the sharing economy exposes companies to greater risk of losing customers or being removed from supply chains.

At the same time, customers are changing what they value, how they value it, and when and where they consume it. It's much harder for businesses to differentiate their offering in more crowded, complicated, and dynamic marketplaces. As such, marketing strategies from just a few years ago can't keep up with the pace of reinvention, forcing organisations to constantly evolve their ways of communicating and delivering value to their prospective and existing customers.

Impact 10: Changing customer behaviours

Evolving definition of product value

Historically, companies created products, then marketing told audiences about those products, focusing on specific features or points of comparison to differentiate their offering and drive sales. However, consumers now look for products and brands that reflect their values and behaviours – and that reinforce deeper connections in every interaction. They expect organisations to be trustworthy and 'be on their side' throughout the relationship, making their lives easier, rather than selling them products they neither want nor need. Customers want to feel like their voices are heard and that they can shape the value they receive.

In fact, consumer purchasing decisions are increasingly driven by emotional connections, rather than by objective logic. Regardless of whether products are cheaper, have more features, or are easier to use, customers are gravitating to the organisation or brand that strikes the strongest emotional chord with them.

The comparison of Apple and other PC offerings is a commonly used example of this, and for good reason. Arguably, Apple's feature specifications are falling behind their competitors' offerings, with fewer device choices, less powerful processors, and significantly higher costs. Yet their market share and brand remain strong, courtesy of a comprehensive native ecosystem, strong design, and an unwavering focus on user experience.

Additionally, 'social value' now plays a far more important role in purchasing decisions. A 2017 study of 20,000 adults from five countries found that 33% of consumers choose to buy from brands that are doing social or environmental good.[2] The report estimated a $1.2 trillion opportunity for brands that make their sustainability credentials clear. Indeed, many brands are already shifting their marketing focus to emphasise their social conscience.

> Patagonia, the outdoor apparel company, launched a US campaign called 'The President Stole Your Land' to highlight the importance of protecting public land[3] and Volvo is investing in ocean waste clean-up and a commitment to making 25% of its cars out of recycled materials by 2025.[4]

Now, consumers are increasingly focused on lifetime relationships rather than tactical transactions. They no longer form perceptions based on a single interaction, but on the full experience with the brand across all touchpoints, creating associations and conclusions that impact their loyalty and engagement. The sum of this collective experience influences all of their buying decisions, requiring companies to develop consistently positive experiences before, during, and after purchase.

> Zappos is well known for creating experiences that improve its customers' lives, from paying tolls on a road on Thanksgiving weekend to a record-breaking ten-hour call to help a customer buy some boots.[5]

From passive to active

In the digital age, customers have far more control. According to Cristina Ziliani, Associate Professor of Marketing at the University of Parma, customers are well-informed, always online, always pressed for time, take non-linear shopping journeys, are exposed to endless choice, have low attention spans, and expect the best price, quality, and experience.[6] They have higher expectations, are harder to satisfy, and more active in sharing their opinions. With independent information and opinion just a click away, they are more informed and powerful and less likely to put up with bewildering choices. Ultimately, organisations can no longer rely on consumer apathy to retain customers.

In addition, customers now own the conversation. They define the topic and won't tolerate bland or generic responses that don't answer their questions. They own the timing, not only expecting an answer as quickly as possible with the least effort on their part, but also finishing the conversation at a pace that suits them. They expect conversations to flow, regardless of their stage in the process or the representative they're speaking to, and they expect organisations to have immediate access to all previous interactions so they don't have to repeat information throughout the process.

Customers also decide the channels they communicate through. Most consumers have several interconnected devices within arm's reach at all times. They have different channel preferences, from social media platforms to email, instant messaging and phone, reflecting how they like to communicate in various scenarios. Importantly, they use *their* channels of choice to communicate – regardless of whether the company is listening or even on that channel. And they don't bend their preferences to align with a company's existing assets or accommodate the CMO's investment plans.

Finally, customers control their journey, regularly moving between channels, platforms, and devices. Their journey is much more complicated than in the past, taking unexpected twists and turns as they change their mind, buy new products during customer service enquiries, or change account preferences during an impulse purchase. This makes it not only harder to track channel effectiveness (especially if organisations are organised in silos and reporting is duplicated by multiple departments taking credit for the same event), but even harder to drive consistent and meaningful engagement.

Demand for greater transparency and authenticity

These days, customers want to know a lot more about the companies they interact with and purchase from. They want 'their' companies to be more human, relatable, and reflective of their own purpose and values. They expect much more transparency from these organisations, so they can make value judgements that build trust and loyalty, while blocking out companies that are opaque or obscure the truth.

According a 2016 study, 78% of customers consider brand transparency to be "very important" and 70% devote extra time to finding out more about the organisations they buy from (Label Insight Transparency ROI).[7] Transparency also drives lifelong loyalty, with 56% of those surveyed saying they would be loyal for life if a company provided complete transparency.[8]

Consumer demand for authenticity and honesty now requires companies to proactively communicate far more about their business. Instead of just product features, consumers want to know what materials went into the products, where they came from, who made them, how they were manufactured, and how sustainable they are. They want to know who is delivering their services, what values guide their behaviour, what the culture is, and how well the workers are treated. They want to know what companies stand for, their purpose and value systems, and their ethical standpoint on social and environmental issues.

Transparency is conspicuous by its absence, and reputations are damaged, sometimes fatally, when information is not readily available or is supressed. A lack of transparency in companies increases their risk of losing control of the positioning narrative – as consumers hunt down missing information online, reaching out to third-party sources to gather facts and opinions.

> Shares in General Motors dropped 16% when an 11-year delay in recalling faulty ignition switches was uncovered in 2014.[9] Subduing information is even worse. The Weinstein Company filed for bankruptcy within months of supressing news about Harvey Weinstein[10], and Oxfam lost 7,000 regular donors in 2018 when news hit that it had supressed reports of staff sexually exploiting victims of the 2010 Haiti earthquake.[11]

Consumers are increasingly demanding data transparency to establish trust with a company or service provider. They are also less likely to share their own data – the lifeblood of targeted promotions – if they don't trust that organisation to look after it. Indeed, one report suggests that customers place a far higher value on the handling of customer data than organisations do themselves.[12]

> The Ranking Digital Rights 2018 Corporate Accountability Index found that "not one of 22 (global) internet, mobile and telecommunications companies earned a privacy score higher than 63%, indicating that most organisations fail to disclose enough information about data privacy to customers."[13]

Impact summary: Changing customer behaviours

Consumers are increasingly motivated by more holistic, fluid, and emotive definitions of value. More than ever, they are increasingly in control of the time, place, and nature of how they extract that value – and are much more demanding of the companies that offer them products and services.

Impact 11: Fragmenting marketplaces

More crowded, competitive markets

The past decade has seen huge growth in the number of channels, particularly with the rise of social media. Facebook, LinkedIn, and Twitter have been joined by Instagram, Pinterest, WhatsApp, Snapchat, and Tumblr. New approaches such as content marketing, search engine optimisation (SEO), and search engine marketing (SEM) have evolved to take advantage of the technology boom, creating more routes to market. At the same time, customers have become multi-channel users, switching regularly between platforms, and making it hard for organisations to know which channels are the most effective.

The proliferation of channels has led to a boom in content.

> In 2017, Smart Insights reported that in just 60 seconds, there are 3.3 million new Facebook posts, 29 million WhatsApp messages, 448,800 tweets, 500 hours of video posted on YouTube, and 3.8 million Google searches.[14]

With all of this information, consumers are at the risk of content overload. Mark Schaefer described this as "content shock" – where there's too much content for audiences to read.[15] As online marketplaces get more crowded and noisier, consumers have started using ad blockers or become 'ad blind', ignoring content and consciously (or subconsciously) screening out information, making it much harder for businesses to get their messages across.[16]

If that weren't enough, increased competition makes it harder for traditional companies to sustain market relevance. New economic and business models are allowing innovative competitors to disrupt existing marketplaces, often with different success criteria that challenge established propositions, positioning, and messaging. Just look at the way Spotify revolutionised music streaming by overcoming the legal challenges of consumers accessing tens of millions of songs[17], and Uber's success, which came from addressing customer needs that traditional taxi or car services initially couldn't meet.[18]

Harder to reach more dispersed, autonomous customers

In addition, traditional marketing approaches are less effective at reaching and engaging customers. As organisations gain access to richer demographic and psychographic (personality/lifestyle) information, the number and variety of audience segments has expanded. As customers expect more personalised communications, generic broadcast marketing approaches deliver diminishing returns. As technology advances and consumers expect a two-way dialogue with vendors whenever and wherever it suits them, information and communication must flow across an ever-expanding 'digital mesh'.[19]

Audiences are atomising. As organisations develop more detailed digital customer profiles to understand their customers, they have also defined more audience segments to target them more effectively. This has inadvertently led to the creation of more markets that organisations have to address with more distinct differentiators. Businesses now need to regularly reframe their value propositions, update their positioning statements, and refresh their messaging for each of these fragmenting segments to ensure that their offering resonates.

The power of one-way mass-market promotions is declining. Consumers can watch the same TV programmes on their devices without the ads, read the same magazine content without choking on perfume samples, or listen to the same music without annoying interruptions.

Traditional advertising is less effective as consumers switch from adverts to AdWords – and 'spray and pray' promotions that target the most consumers fail to engage more demanding audiences. While offline media does play a role, with TV and print still delivering strong ROI, their traditional mass-market reach is reducing as consumers gravitate towards their preferred digital channels, paying to *avoid* advertising.

This also means that when organisations do try to connect with their audiences, their marketing communications have to flow seamlessly across an increasingly complicated web of smart machines, people, and systems. Each client or customer is increasingly hyperconnected, expecting immediate and slick experiences on constantly evolving technologies and formats. Messages have to be mobile-enabled, automatically adjusting to different operating systems, screen sizes, and devices. Communications need to be two-way, allowing business to enter into dialogue with customers anywhere and at any time.

Constantly differentiated offerings

To remain relevant, successful enterprises are regularly updating each offering's proposition, promotion, and delivery mechanism. They are adapting their marketing approaches to meet more fluid customer buying criteria, moving their promotions away from assessments of functional fit at fixed points in time – towards dynamic, multi-faceted reflections of long-term value.

Customers and clients now base their buying decisions on a wider, more demanding set of buying criteria. They have more access to more information and more options to choose from, increasing the range of product qualities they assess. Their needs are more fluid and harder to predict, making it trickier for companies to clearly define their requirements. Consumers now assess values, behaviours, and social good as much as cost, convenience, and quality. For business buyers, decision-making authority is increasingly devolved to larger groups of stakeholders with wider sets of requirements.

Once purchased, product and service differentiators have to be reinforced throughout the ownership lifespan. Customers expect better lifetime experiences and to see differentiators reinforced before, during, and long after the actual purchasing decision. Technology firms that provided free software updates after the point of purchase set a customer expectation that all industries are now accountable to. Customers want their decisions constantly validated, directly through interactions with the vendor and indirectly through peer networks or information platforms.

Finally, customers expect offerings to evolve to meet their changing circumstances. They don't expect to start a new buying journey for a brand-new product each time their situation changes. They are aware that their needs will change over time and expect that the products and services they have already bought will evolve with them to meet those demands. This is especially relevant for B2B businesses that have longer product lifecycles and more subscription-based business models, increasing the expectation that solutions will dynamically evolve over the course of the relationship.

Impact summary: Fragmenting marketplaces

As markets are becoming more crowded and complicated, audiences fragment and disperse, making them harder to reach. Products and services need to be constantly differentiated, and businesses have to work harder to make their offerings known, let alone meet customer expectations. As a result, companies can no longer rely on one-way mass-market promotions to connect with demanding consumers, while pressure is mounting on them to regularly update their offerings to remain relevant.

Impact 12: The demand for richer, personalised communication

Shift from push to pull

Traditional 'push' marketing approaches – where core product messages are broadcast to many – are being replaced by 'pull' marketing methods – where companies seek to influence their customers indirectly through social media, third parties, and external influencers. Pull marketing tries to establish a loyal following to draw consumers to their products, strengthening awareness and therefore demand.

Reputations are increasingly critical, and relationships between forward-thinking companies and their customers are characterised as bi-lateral peer-to-peer (P2P) exchanges, where customer experiences are more personalised and appropriate online content is immediately available to them.

As customers change from passive to active, organisations are developing more targeted promotions to reach and engage them. Technology has powered the growth of hyper-personalisation, using browsing, purchasing, and real-time behavioural data to tailor promotions for each user. Each customer has their own device, which in turn provides additional layers of contextual insight to companies on customer behaviours. In return for supplying more personal data on their purchasing patterns, customers expect intimate, tailored, and richer experiences.

This has led to an explosion in the demand for bespoke, relevant content, which has become essential to create the experiences that connect consumers with products and brands. In an age of information overload, consumers tend not to remember specific products, but they do remember the experiences they have with brands. Organisations are now required to produce more and more tailored content in the form of pictures, videos, podcasts, whitepapers, or infographics just to maintain awareness and relevance.

At the same time, promotion has transformed from distribution to access. Businesses are seeing the decline of 'one to many' communication approaches and the growth of 'many to one' and 'many to many'. To cut through the noise, content now needs to be contextualised for each platform that consumers prefer to use and curated for relevance and impact.

The growing power of self-discovery

Indirect communication channels are now playing a much more significant role in how organisations communicate and deliver offerings for their customers. Effective promotion is becoming less about what organisations say to their customers and more about what customers say to each other. Customers prefer to find and learn about new brands themselves, favouring self-discovery via personal recommendations, browsing in store, or online search engines.

Social media is a key battleground to reach and influence these proactive audiences.

Currently, Americans spend an average of 23.6 hours online every week, and most of that is on social media,[20] while 40% of users use social platforms to follow their favourite brands.[21]

The inherent sharing capability of social technology enables customers to discover information faster, and its personal nature means they can circumvent traditional sales and marketing functions and ask direct questions. This also allows them to connect with like-minded others, enabling them to force changes in products, services, and even brands.

Social media is also enabling a new type of influencer to rise to prominence. B2C companies are less dependent on celebrity endorsement and B2B no longer relies on client lists to validate their offering. Consumers are disengaging from corporate advertising – and in its place, ordinary people with personal credibility are filling the void.

> SAP, the ERP software company, works with third-party influencers such as independent consultants, academics, and authors to create relevant content that promote SAP's services. GE has set up an influencer marketing campaign working with Lena Dunham's feminist online publication *Lenny Letter* to help with its recruitment efforts.[22]

Third-party ratings have become a vital part of the purchase journey. Consumers are increasingly turning to each other instead of companies to verify the quality and accuracy of products and services offered online. Third-party ratings not only enable consumers to mitigate the risk of not physically checking the product themselves, but also provide an objective, relevant review of how the product relates to them. They provide a level of social proof that informs buying decisions, removing a bit of uncertainty.[23] For example, Amazon's star rating system allows consumers to quickly evaluate the popularity and perceived quality of products.

Always on, everywhere

Before the digital age, there were defined windows for customers and clients to buy offerings and limited options for them to interact with vendors. Now, the options for communication at every stage of the consumer lifecycle seem almost limitless. The disciplines of marketing, selling, and customer service are converging as customers define the channel, conversation, and journey. Organisations need to be always on everywhere, monitoring multiple channels and responding immediately and intelligently to a greater variety of requests at more stages of the customer lifecycle.

Customers have more choice in how they communicate. In addition to email and phone, technology enables them to communicate directly through webforms, which plug into websites and CRM systems. Customers and organisations can converse using SMS and apps, while chatrooms and social media have opened up multiple indirect channels where clients and consumers can ask questions. Many connected consumers are not mobile-first, but mobile-only. Organisations have to be available on the channels that customers currently choose, and monitor the accelerating development of new platforms to ensure they stay one step ahead of demand.

The variety, volume, and velocity of customer interactions has rocketed. Social networks such as Twitter and Facebook allow consumers to directly approach organisations for free – day or night, while mobile devices enable the public to communicate whenever and wherever they are, rapidly increasingly the volume of questions business need to respond to. Digital technology has enabled consumers to be more vocal, sharing more opinions both with organisations and their personal networks, and opening up a wider variety of channels for them to make more pre-sales enquiries.[24]

Consumers and clients increasingly expect an intelligent relationship with brands, and if they don't get it, it's easy for them to take their money elsewhere. Instant access to knowledge has changed customer perceptions of what is acceptable and what isn't. Customers know that companies have their data and can easily identify them when they log in to web properties, use their apps, email, or call them.

> According to Vala Afshar, Chief Digital Evangelist at Salesforce and author of the book *The Pursuit of Social Business Excellence* (Charles Pinot, 2012), customers now expect every touchpoint to be immediate, personalised, and proactive. Afshar's research of 7,000 consumers and business buyers worldwide indicated that 65% of consumers expect companies to interact with them in real time, with 80% stating that a company responding immediately influences their loyalty.[25]

Impact summary: Richer, personalised communication

It is much more complicated for organisations to effectively communicate their proposition. The digital age has seen a shift from media defined by production (press, radio, TV) to content defined by users, changing how businesses create demand and build trust. A requirement for greater intimacy is driving consumers towards new channels and sources of information, which is forcing businesses to update their approaches to promotion and awareness. As attention spans drop and demand for instant gratification increases, organisations must develop new ways to deliver offerings to their audiences.

Optimising in the digital age

To succeed in this changing world, organisations have to shift their approach to positioning. They need to develop deeper consumer relationships that enhance their understanding of changing demand, repositioning themselves as life-long trusted partners that dynamically meet their customers' requirements. Demand has to be created in entirely new ways, improving the lives of consumers so that they in turn are more likely to renew their commitment while recommending products and services to their own networks. Connections with customers have to be constantly reinforced and experiences actively reshaped to meet growing customer expectations.

Recommendation 10: Reposition in the lives, not the minds of customers

Treat customers as users, not buyers

Think of customers less as one-time buyers of specific products and services – and more as members you have a long-term relationship with. A joint study by SAP, Siegel+Gale, and ShiftThinking suggests that successful businesses **focus on creating demand to *use* products, rather than *buy* them**, shaping how consumers experience the brand in every part of the customer journey.[26] Instead of selling, organisations should seek to create a compelling, consistent, and benevolent ecosystem that enables continuous and mutual success.

> Apple is an obvious success story here, having built an interconnected ecosystem including iPhones, iTunes, and iCloud that encourages ongoing and deepening usage, while discouraging the use of non-native products. Many customers have become lifelong fans: brand ambassadors who will spread the word. Apple stores have removed checkout areas and placed the Genius Bar in prominent areas to help existing customers deepen their connection with (and dependency on) their products and services.

Secondly, marketing teams should **think outside the sales funnel**. Traditional marketing tends to focus exclusively on the buying cycle, pushing 'interested' consumers along the path to purchase. However, organisations need to spend as much, if not *more*, time on the post-purchase experience to develop broader insights that underpin long-term brand relevance and deepen customer loyalty.

Organisations should extend their customer experience design approach into every part of their customer lifecycle to identify critical touchpoints that shape engagement.

> Tesla's customer experience approach led to the creation of Mobile Service Rangers who travel to customers' homes to perform post-purchase inspections and upgrades, while their Tesla Stores around the world have been repositioned as a private network of VIP members' lounges.[27]

Finally, reorient relevant teams to **treat customers like assets that will grow in value**. Instead of targeting the highest-value sales, bewildering clients with information, or charging for what they might not want, organisations should position themselves as collaborative partners that empower their customers' continued success.

> Salesforce disrupted the CRM market by positioning itself as a cost-effective partner against Siebel's higher-priced, more complex on-premise applications. Leveraging Software as a Service (SaaS), customers could subscribe to its software without significant capital expenditure while benefiting from regular functionality upgrades based on real-time customer feedback.[28]

Focus on relationships, trust and transparency

As a growing proportion of customer lifetime value is driven after the initial sale, focus on expanding relationships to keep your customers for longer.[29] Build deeper emotional connections to develop loyalty and underpin advocacy. Simultaneously encourage consumer feedback so you can improve the development of offerings, capturing more detailed and contextualised input to reduce the risks to product innovation. Be proactively transparent, pre-empting potential questions or concerns from stakeholders.

As brand and experience increasingly become one and the same for consumers, your marketing, sales and customer relationship teams should work closely to **develop valuable, consistent, and congruent experiences throughout the customer lifecycle**. Encourage closer relationships between product development and marketing to tie products and brand closer together. Invest in customer relationship departments who will spend more time listening to customers and sharing insights across the expanded team. Ensure that design thinking is applied between functional teams, not just within.

As markets accelerate and competition increases, it's even more important for organisations to focus on demand, not supply. While many businesses already put the customer at the centre, competitive advantage comes from *actively* **working with customers to unlock the potential in the relationship**.

More than just embedding the voice of the customer, focus on developing bilateral customer relationships that actively involve clients in product roadmaps, encourage involvement in new product development, or voice insights into future challenges. Encourage your senior leaders to dedicate regular and significant time to engage directly with consumers and clients, instead of relying on requests for customer surveys.

As consumers are increasingly motived by sustainability, purpose, and social good, **communicate and reinforce your company's values-based credentials**. Incentivise teams to give customers what they want, not charge them for things they don't need. Be transparent in the data you collect, why you're collecting it, what you're going to do with it, and how you're securely storing it and complying with evolving data laws. Be open about your operations and embed high ethical standards across the supply chain.

Zappos has created an extranet to give all of its vendors complete visibility into its business, and Patagonia has launched a project called 'Footprint Chronicles' to provide transparency about its supply chain and ensure it has no negative social or environmental impacts.[30]

Dynamic repositioning

Markets are constantly shifting and adapting to accelerating forces of change. New technology creates new opportunities and threats, new competitors enter the field, and consumer tastes change. Instead of just positioning products, services, and brands at the *beginning* of their lifecycle, create processes, systems, and behaviours that *continually* reposition products and services throughout their lifespan to maximise their relevance to key consumers.

Try setting up **regular reviews of brand position against consumer perception**. Map customer journeys and frequently measure their experience at each touchpoint. A brand positioning audit (ideally by an independent third party) unpicks how customers see the brand and measures the specific differences between intended and actual perceptions. The audit results can also help businesses to reframe their value proposition and update their positioning statements – ensuring that their offering continues to resonate effectively with each target audience.

In addition, **constantly track and highlight the product qualities that customers value the most**. As markets evolve, so do the product or service attributes that are in demand. The Kano model can help define the product features and customer satisfaction of each attribute, ranging from one-dimensional qualities like battery life on a laptop to the attractive qualities that create excitement and long-term engagement.[31] Forecast the evolving attributes that are most important to customers, then distinguish these qualities in your products and services during your promotion efforts, as well as factoring them into ongoing product development initiatives.

Finally, **simplify and refresh your customer propositions**. Remember, increasing market fragmentation has increased the complexity of choice for consumers. They have less time or inclination to wade through bewildering lists of product features and specifications. Instead, encourage marketing teams to simplify messaging, making it easier to digest and recall, and make products and services easy to use.

> For example, IBM successfully streamlined their range of quantum computing offers through their 'Smarter Planet' approach.

Recommendation summary: Lives not minds

While many traditional companies position their brands in the minds of consumers, successful organisations position them in the lives of consumers. Engage customers more as users than as buyers, shifting your investments to improve experiences outside the sales funnel. Focus on creating deeper, productive, long-term relationships, building trust and engagement through proactive transparency. At the same time, constantly update your propositions and promotions to remain dynamically relevant to demanding audiences.

Recommendation 11: Give more to get more

Provide experiences and content that will make customers' lives better

As consumers shift from buyers to users, create demand by showing, not telling, customers how your products and services make them successful. Using the example of a makeup department in a large store, Mark Bonchek and Vivek Bapat describe traditional marketing as "getting customers to buy the product with samples and professional makeovers. By contrast, new marketing approaches provide instruction, community, and services to help people feel confident in being able to use the products themselves when they get home."[32]

Start by **getting customers involved in the development of relevant and compelling content**. Use online surveys or focus groups to tap into the key motivations and issues that matter to them. Ask trusted customers directly what content would help them achieve their goals or what they want to discover. Dive deep into search trends and social conversations, using analytics tools to see which words or phrases visitors are using most online. Source ideas from frontline employees who interact with customers every day. Request and share user-generated content and customer stories to contextualise your offering and add authenticity and credibility.

Next, **target consumers with the content and experiences that matter most to them**. As content builds, audit and categorise it into key user requirements (such as informative, educational, thought leadership, entertaining, thought-provoking, or socially valuable). Classify content further for different touchpoints across the customer lifecycle. For example, long-term customers and new prospects may be engaged by different types of thought leadership. Configure the content for each platform to improve sharing and discoverability. By aligning content to existing audience profiles, organisations can quickly distribute relevant, engaging content to the right customer segments.

Finally, focus on **quality of experience at emotionally charged 'moments of truth.'**[33] Certain experiences in the customer lifecycle are significantly more important than others – attracting deeper emotional investment from customers and greater opportunity and risk for vendors. For example, when a customer has a problem with a large online financial transaction or is trying to book an urgent last-minute flight.

Within customer experience design, identify the interactions that are most important to your consumers and empower frontline human capital to put customers' needs ahead of policy compliance or rigid workflows. Additionally, identify and address the practices that drive negative moments of truth, such as aggressive sales behaviour.

Advocacy and influence, not promotion and sales

Shift your teams' focus from promotion and sales to advocacy and influence. Peer-to-peer endorsements have become essential, not only in sparking self-discovery but also increasing trust in a brand as being relevant and reliable. Encourage your marketing leaders to create a self-sustaining customer ecosphere that fosters intimacy and authenticity, generating continuous interest, demand, and advocacy.

Target your customer-facing teams to **build strong, loyal communities** who are deeply engaged and happy to recommend. Communities generate qualitative feedback to continually innovate products, identify key market trends and make your customers feel like their voices matter. Start out by identifying the type of community you want. This should reflect your brand purpose and values, and be appealing and valuable to target customers: for example, aligning around a common interest or acting as a support group.

Next, research similar communities to understand how they engage with members and what content they share, then identify any gaps to exploit. Create positive feedback loops with content generation, listening to concerns and incorporating elements back into messages. Actively manage these communities, monitor their conversations, and find ways to bring them together offline, if possible, to deepen engagement.

Additionally, ensure that some of your promotions **'tell your story'**. Storytelling brings meaning, inspiration, and emotional connection. As Simon Sinek outlined in his TED talk 'How Great Leaders Inspire Action'[34] storytelling helps companies to articulate their purpose, appealing directly to the limbic part of the brain that controls decision-making and behaviour.

Stories connect customers (and employees) to brands in deeper ways, creating loyalty and advocacy while using the richer language of common humanity and shared purpose. Ensure that your teams leverage authentic stories that encapsulate your purpose and values, sharing challenges and difficulties as well as successes.

Finally, encourage your business to **partner with authentic influencers**. Consumers prefer to discover new products and services from the sources they trust the most, particularly personal recommendations. They are increasingly turning to third-party influencers to shape their purchasing habits. However, not all recommendations are equal, with bought endorsements from bloggers or third parties the least effective sources of brand discovery. Instead, make sure your business collaborates with authentic influencers who are individually credible, passionate about their industry, and promote only those products and services they genuinely believe in.

> In the US, Dell partnered with Mike Libecki from National Geographic to showcase its 'Rugged' range of technology in a natural and authentic setting.[35]

Focus on customer success

The success of a business is inherently intertwined with the success of its customers. If customers succeed using a company's products and services, they'll continue to use them – creating a virtuous cycle.[36] The deeper a business understands their customers' desired outcomes, the closer they can match their offerings to evolving needs, the longer customers stay, and the more they will pay. So, invest in a "proactive, holistic and organisation-level approach to customer success to ensure consumers continually and increasingly receive value over the course of the customer lifetime".[37]

First, **step inside your customers' experience to understand their perspective**.

Observe customers in a natural setting, exploring their real-time experiences and understanding their behaviours and attitudes in various situations. Be clear on customer expectations of the experience (unmet expectations will always deliver a poor experience regardless of the effort put in) and prioritise engagement measures rather than ad impressions or customer satisfaction (CSAT) scores. Step into your customers' shoes, as this will help you quickly identify the barriers to their success and identify potential solutions.

Make customer success a strategic goal. Sales and marketing alone are not enough to sustain growth as customer acquisition costs accelerate and customers switch more regularly and easily. Reposition your customer relationship efforts less as a risk-management cost centre and more as a growth engine that proactively helps consumers derive maximum value from your products and services.

Develop an organisation-wide customer success programme to define strategic objectives, funding models, and resources. Incorporate a customer success philosophy and metrics within the overall business plan – incentivising and aligning internal and external human capital on customer value creation, not transactional task completion. Define a unified go-to-market model that designates clear responsibilities throughout the customer lifecycle while underwriting cross-functional collaboration.

Finally, **upskill existing customer-facing teams**. Rather than hiring more customer service representatives, invest time and effort into evolving the capability of your current human capital. Customer success teams have long delivered cost-effective growth in many software vendors, combining product knowledge, domain expertise, and intimate customer knowledge to spot opportunities, proactively solve problems, and effectively coordinate internal resources.

McKinsey recommends building a talent engine that develops training and education programmes based on top-performing customer success managers – simultaneously leveraging advanced analytics to help customer success teams focus on key differentiators.[38]

Recommendation summary: Give more to get more

Focus on creating demand for use, rather than purchase of your products and services, throughout the customer lifecycle. To drive engagement, prioritise experiences and content above broadcast messaging and lead generation, and shift from direct promotion to indirect advocacy and influence. Rather than focusing on short-term sales targets, focus on customers' long-term success to drive renewals, additional revenue per user, and customer advocacy.

Recommendation 12: Bridge the gap

Omnipresent

Omni-channel customer experiences rely on organisations being omnipresent. Business should be available 24/7 on all channels to enable direct relationships with the end users of their products and services.

Start by **developing a flexible customer operations infrastructure** that combines the most appropriate new tools while leveraging legacy systems. The next chapter on operational excellence explores ways to bridge the gap between large enterprise systems and the latest technology solutions to create the best customer experiences.

Alongside those efforts, leaders should augment systems to deepen and strengthen customer relationships. For example, automation can execute and manage campaigns or respond to enquiries around the clock – freeing up teams to focus on higher-value activity or track customer journeys more effectively between the connected web of devices.

At the same time, businesses should **leverage their existing operational ecosystems**, building on current touchpoints to improve their connection with new and existing customers. For example, Amazon successfully extended their book ecosystem to connect customers to a wider range of products. Capitalise on relationships with suppliers, distributors, retailers, industry associations, institutional partners, and government agencies to develop mutually beneficial collaborations that connect and engage new and existing audiences.

Proactively listen and respond to deliver superior experiences

Now businesses are able to foster direct relationships with end users, ensure that your teams are empowered to engage them in authentic ways on the right channels at the right time. Leverage your new digital ecosystem to ensure that you don't miss the moments of truth that can transform an indifferent consumer into a lifelong advocate. Get ahead of the problem, proactively guiding customers and positively shaping relationships while reducing customer effort.

Ensure that customer-facing **teams treat everything like it matters**. When customers have a poor experience with an organisation, they are less likely to do business with them and more likely to tell their network. As customers become users, these experiences matter at every point in the customer lifecycle.

Map out all of the important customer journeys – highlighting the technology and processes needed and the teams required to deliver them. Identify critical steps within each journey and establish reporting mechanisms to quickly flag customer challenges to the appropriate teams (in the next chapter, we'll also look at using proactive monitoring tools). These should include parts of the customer experience that have traditionally been overlooked, such as order fulfilment or invoicing. Finally, deploy your newly trained customer success teams to proactively focus on the key challenges highlighted by the reporting.

Focus on social listening to understand what your audience has to say about your business, your competitors, and the market. Social listening provides data and insights to know your customers better and feedback loops to improve products and services. Importantly, it can help you create wonderful customer experiences to powerfully position brands with customers. Consider using free tools such as Hootsuite, which has great social media management functions, or Brandwatch Analytics, which offers customisable query-builders and dashboards.

Use technology to get ahead of problems, optimising customer experiences while pre-empting challenges. Customers are less tolerant of being forced to contact suppliers about known problems, repeatedly identify themselves on connected devices associated with their account, or fit around suppliers' fault-resolution schedules. Instead, businesses should leverage technology to proactively solve problems, for example, guiding customers through interactive troubleshooting sessions as soon as an issue is detected. Organisations can also use context engines to track and correlate interactions from different channels; and devices to analyse the overall customer journey and make recommendations to improve their experience.

Fast data to enrich personalisation and delivery

The information revolution is producing a mass of data that is transforming the way companies engage with and inspire their customers. However, just collecting data is not enough. Focus on constantly extrapolating insights from that data, empowering teams to take immediate action to improve experiences.

Use the data to **understand your individual customers**, gaining insights to create the experiences that matter to them. Develop a broader, more balanced picture of each customer – not to only understand what they're doing, but to better understand who your customers truly are. Customer-insight programs help you integrate and make sense of all sources of customer insights, both formal and informal. Insight communities bring perspective and consumer needs back into the product development process.[39]

Mine your data, using software to look for patterns to learn more about your customers. There's a wealth of information filtering in from omni-channel customers all the time, and business need to dig through all of the unsolicited data to build a full picture of the customer experience. Many tools out there can help.

For example, natural language processing (NLP) can not only spot large-scale trends, but also evaluate the real-time effectiveness of each part of the supply chain. Sentiment analysis measures the emotion behind customer engagement, enabling businesses to improve customer empathy and build stronger two-way relationships.

Finally, set up simple **real-time customer metrics and dashboards**. The most effective metrics deliver insights quickly, so businesses can rapidly act on them. Ensure they are delivered in a way that decision-makers can quickly understand – and make sure they forecast future opportunities, not just report on past activity. Set up metrics to flow in real time to key decision-makers across the business, and ensure that dashboards empower creative delivery, rather than overloading leaders with too much data.

Recommendation summary: Bridge the gap

The pressure on operational delivery is increasing as organisations struggle to keep pace with evolving consumer behaviour, atomising marketplaces, and the demand for richer, more personalised communication. Businesses need to "bridge the expanding divide between what customers expect and what they get" not just to better connect with consumers, but to actively shape their interactions.[40] Invest in systems, technology, and analytics that utilise speed to meet client demands before competitors, context to deliver on promises in the most appropriate manner, and insights to respond instantly and intelligently to customer needs.

Positioning for Success

IMPACT OF FORCES

I10. *Changing customer behaviours*	**I11.** *Fragmenting marketplaces*	**I12.** *Demand for richer, personalised communication*
Evolving definition of product value • Emotional connection more powerful than product features • Increasing importance of 'social value' • Shift to lifetime relationships from transactional exchanges	**More crowded, competitive markets** • More channels • More content • More competition	**Shift from push to pull** • Demand for greater personalisation • More tailored, more relevant content • Promotion shift from distribution to access
From passive to active • Customers own the conversation • They decide the channel • They control the journey	**Harder to reach more dispersed, autonomous customers** • Atomising audiences • Power of one-way mass-market promotions declining • Messages must flow across complicated web of devices, people, and systems	**Growing power of self-discovery** • Social media key battleground • Rise of new breed of influencers • Power of third-party ratings
Demand greater transparency and authenticity • Want to know everything • Transparency conspicuous by its absence • Data transparency central to digital trust	**Constantly differentiated offerings** • Wider, more demanding set of buying criteria • Throughout ownership lifespan • Offerings expected to evolve to meet changing circumstances	**Always on, everywhere** • More consumer choice over how to communicate • Variety, volume, and velocity of customer interactions rocketed • Expect interactions to be instant and intelligent

RECOMMENDATIONS   ACTIVATE ➤

ACTIVATE

R10. *Reposition in lives, not minds, of customers*	**R11.** *Give more to get more*	**R12.** *Bridge the gap*
Treat customers as users, not buyers • Create demand to use, not buy • Think outside the sales funnel • Treat customers as assets that will grow in value	**Provide experiences that makes customers' lives better** • Involve customers in content creation • Target with experiences that add the most value to them • Focus on quality of experience at emotionally charged moments of truth	**Omnipresent** • Flexible customer operations infrastructure • Leverage existing ecosystems
Focus in relationships, trust and transparency • Develop valuable, consistent, and congruent experiences • Actively unlock the potential in customer relationships • Proactively communicate values-based credentials	**Advocacy and Influence, not promotion and sales** • Focus on building strong, loyal communities • Tell your story • Partner with *authentic* influencers	**Proactively listen and respond to deliver superior experiences** • Treat everything like it matters • Focus on social listening • Use technology to get ahead of customer issues
Dynamic repositioning • Regular reviews of brand position against perception • Track and highlight most valued product qualities • Simplify and refresh customer propositions	**Focus on 'customer success'** • Step inside customer experience • Make customer success a strategic goal • Upskill existing customer-facing teams	**Fast data to enrich personalisation and delivery** • Understand individual customers • Mine your data • Real-time customer metrics and dashboards

CHAPTER 8

Operational Excellence

Business operations focus on the everyday activities and commitments that deliver the strategy. This includes how a product or service is produced, how customer orders are fulfilled, how costs are controlled, and how quality is maintained. It's the job of operations to "optimise assets under financial constraints, meeting and exceeding customer expectations and supporting it through relevant technology".[1]

Traditionally, operations focus on efficiency, improving the day-to-day management of what an organisation does to increase speed and reduce waste. The aim is to improve the ratio of useful work performed to total effort made. Operations also focus on risk, attempting to reduce an organisation's exposure to transactional hazards by reducing the probability and amount of loss within workflows.

Operations and strategy are in a symbiotic relationship. While strategy defines the steps, activities, and methods that a business takes to achieve its long-term goals, operations keeps the machinery of the business operating at peak levels. Strategy cannot work without operations – no amount of strategic positioning matters if an organisation is unable to deliver on its promises.

Similarly, operations cannot work without strategy, as actions become just a series of interconnected tasks that almost certainly can't deliver intended results. Operations also work alongside structure and leadership, providing the detailed information and practices that empower workflows, systems, and teams.

Why should leaders care?

Good operations improve margins, enhance customer engagement, and help profitability. Great operations create distinctive differentiators at each step of the value chain to deliver competitive advantage. Operations can reduce the cost of doing business, increase the value to the customer, improve the quality of the product or service, and increase the margin it can be sold for. Operations can also improve supply-chain management and re-engineer processes to dramatically improve speed and agility.

As such, operations are fundamental to commercial success. Toyota developed Just-In-Time (JIT) ordering and delivery, plus lean manufacturing and supply, to dramatically improve their performance. McDonald's was founded on operational innovation, pioneering assembly-line food production in the back with customer-focused service at the front. Six Sigma, a quality approach originally developed at Motorola, was successfully applied by Jack Welch to transform manufacturing, service, and administration across General Electric.[2]

Impact of the forces

Analytics, Big Data, the cloud, the Internet of Things, mobile, application development, and other impactful technologies are changing what, when, and how operations deliver value. Operations have to deliver more products and services faster, while the skills required are changing more regularly and more unpredictably. Many existing operational approaches cannot keep up with the speed, volume, or variety of change.

At the same time, evolving risks and liabilities are fundamentally changing the operating realities that businesses have to manage. Operational functions now play a much more critical role in delivering competitive advantage, underwriting customer experience and loyalty, leveraging new technologies, and responding quicker to both opportunities and threats.

Impact 13: Growing pressure on operational functions

Everyday business activities are changing more regularly

The activities and commitments that deliver the strategy not only have a shorter shelf life now, but are subject to frequent iterations. Operational teams have to support products and services that are changing more often, working harder just to maintain existing products – let alone deliver new ones.

> The mobile phone sector is an interesting example. The iconic Nokia 3310 was launched in 2000 and dominated the market with just a few improvements over its eight-year lifetime. In contrast, phone manufacturers now deliver regular updates throughout the year, some with huge variations. Apple launched iOS 12 in 2018 with at least 17 "big new features" added since iOS 11 was released a year earlier.[3]

Operational teams need to continually react to growing external forces. They have to regularly adjust to greater volumes of feedback from demanding customers, while agile competitors continually push up quality standards and push down response times. New laws require modified approaches, be it the EU's General Data Protection Regulation (GDPR) or new regulations such as those applied to the financial markets after the global financial crisis. A growing range of external forces requires operational teams to be increasingly alert and more responsive than ever before.

Everyday business activities have to work much harder and adapt more regularly to maintain customer relationships. As discussed in the previous chapter, the nature and length of customer relationships are changing as distrust grows, customer attention spans drop, and demand changes more regularly. Loyalty is falling – customers are less willing to sign up to long-term contracts and it's easier for them to compare and switch suppliers. Consumer expectations continue to grow, requiring both B2B and B2C organisations to regularly update their customer approach to ensure satisfaction.

Increased operational complexity

As higher levels of outsourcing, expanding contractual requirements, and the demand for greater customisation grows, operational teams are less able to standardise their processes and activities.

Customers now expect less friction and fuss and shorter, higher-value processes when interacting with vendors. Operational teams have to support these customisations, developing extra processes, enabling new ways to communicate, via additional touchpoints, on a greater number of platforms.

An increasingly fragmented supply chain has to be effectively harnessed as businesses become dependent on greater volumes of external specialists for operational capability, capacity, and competence. As the number of independent suppliers grows, operational infrastructures have to support additional processes and procedures to ensure that value can be extracted in the most efficient way. A one-size-fits-all approach is increasingly ineffective as partners become less accepting of the process and policy standardisation associated with vertically integrated businesses.

Operations also need to manage, maintain, and monitor expanded contractual requirements. As customer relationships become progressively explicit, so do the contractual necessities supporting them. Standardised or long-term contracts lack agility for both vendor and buyer, elevating the risks and exposure for both parties. As organisations become reliant on greater volumes of external specialists, managing operational risks is increasingly dependent on specific contractual provisions with a fragmenting group of partners.

Greater operational risks

As demand and complexity grow, many long-established operational certainties are being challenged. Traditional assets are depreciating faster, with some turning into liabilities. Costs are harder to predict and maintain – and incumbent systems, tools, and approaches are struggling to keep up. It's now much harder for operations to maintain financial stability, let alone their operating margin.

Operational infrastructures that carry significant operational expenditure (opex), capital expenditure (capex), and liabilities are increasingly at a disadvantage. Future benefits from assets such as data centres and large manufacturing equipment are falling. As product lifecycles speed up, projected returns from inventory diminish. As discussed in *Chapter 6: Structure and Leadership*, large permanent headcounts and fixed real estate that were once comparative advantages now create operational risk, while restricting agility and cash flow.

At the same time, operational costs have become harder to forecast and control.

Since June 2008 when crude oil hit $162 per barrel, the price has oscillated between $128 in 2011 and $36 in 2016.[4] Between January 2010 and October 2018, UK wholesale electricity prices have varied between £65 and £34 per MWh.[5] Following 15 years of stability, global commodity prices have fluctuated wildly over the past decade, with natural gas falling 23% and zinc falling 29%, while wheat has increased by 11% and propane has jumped by 17%.[6]

Finally, incumbent infrastructures are producing diminishing operational returns. As we explored in *Chapter 1: Political, Economic, and Commercial Instability*, national infrastructures are less able to support the productivity initiatives that many organisations have invested in. Organisations are experiencing declining returns from re-investing in operational frameworks that were devised and installed in a pre-digital age. Systems, tools, processes, and procedures configured to deliver consistency and compliance are now struggling to keep up with the changing pace and nature of demand.

Impact summary: Growing pressure

Operational teams have more to cope with than ever. As customers demand more personalised offerings more frequently, teams must support a wider range of faster changing products and services, which is restricting their ability to standardise processes, systems, and administration. At the same time, risks are rising, undermining the certainties that many operational engines were built on.

Impact 14: Changed operational realities

Focussing on production efficiency increases exposure to disruption

Operational infrastructures have traditionally been configured to deliver production efficiency. However, operational inputs are now much less predictable, let alone controllable, while incremental efficiency does not address the growing demand for constantly evolving, higher-value outputs.

If that wasn't enough, production efficiency can actually increase exposure to disruption from new competitors, new technology, and new business models. Commercial risks grow as operational teams are deflected away from powerful threats and meaningful opportunities. Concentrating on a 1-2% efficiency improvement year on year will not deliver competitive advantage when competitors do the same. Offerings will not be differentiated enough and consumers will not notice any appreciable benefits between suppliers.

As new competitors disrupt established markets, established organisations are increasingly unprotected against the danger of new technology that can rewrite the rules of their industry, and more vulnerable to new business models that can reach their customers in faster, more compelling ways.

Permanent workforces less agile and cost-effective

The increasing demand for the latest specialist skills, growing pressure on costs, and increased operational risks is changing how operations leverage human capital. There is an expanding skills gap between an organisation's fast-evolving commercial strategy and their permanent workforce's ability to keep up. Predominantly permanent workforces are less able to meet the challenges of the digital age.

Accelerating markets not only demand new skills, but require those skills to change more often. While the information revolution is enabling organisations to better forecast the skills and experience they need, traditional recruitment, training, and upskilling approaches that focus on permanent employees simply cannot deliver those skills fast enough.

It's now less cost-effective to permanently acquire or develop specialist skills. Even if skills are available in time from a permanent workforce, they aren't relevant or valuable for as long, increasing both the operational cost and risks to the organisation. In fact, many of today's essential skills become surplus faster due to constantly evolving programming languages, more effective manufacturing approaches, and changing customer demands.

Uneven playing surface

Organisations that have accumulated large fixed assets are at an increasing disadvantage, as their operational costs are inflated compared to new challengers. This turns many fixed assets from a strength to a weakness. At the same time, some organisations are able to ignore the market forces that other enterprises are obliged to follow, distorting market equality.

Different operating and business models have completely different risks and liabilities. As mentioned in *Chapter 1: Political, Economic, and Commercial Instability*, Uber changed the world of taxis without having to buy or maintain fleets of vehicles, enabling them to quickly challenge the incumbent operators in cities around the world. Airbnb changed how the world goes on holiday, without any hotels to manage or local staff to pay.

Challengers are no longer predictable peers, but come from anywhere. These days, benchmarking against known competitors will not necessarily improve operational performance, as they no longer accurately reflect the true marketplace. New competitors are building operational infrastructures around completely different success criteria. Consumer experience is replacing service. Long-term value is replacing cost. Sharing is replacing owning. Operational infrastructures geared to deliver in the pre-digital age are increasingly unable to compete with new organisations configured for a different reality.

Operating rules don't apply consistently to every company. Some organisations can ignore certain risks and liabilities through their existing market dominance. For example, many large technology businesses buy or lease the most expensive real estate, recruit huge numbers of permanent workers, and build up significant fixed assets despite the inflated costs and risks. Indeed, their cash position enables them to take advantage of gaps in the market created by prevailing market conditions, forcing other organisations out.

Others are protected by the state, subsidised to safeguard revenues while external competitors are penalised through tariffs and trade barriers. The latter also restrict access to physical materials, technology, and innovation – limiting access to critical resources for some organisations, but not others.

Impact summary: Changed operational realities

Evolving risks and liabilities are changing how and when operational teams add value. Production efficiency can no longer deliver consistent returns. External on-demand talent is better positioned to deliver value faster than fixed permanent workforces. Established operating rules no longer apply consistently within markets, let alone between them.

Impact 15: Increasingly critical role delivering The Plan

Operations key to positive customer experiences

As falling trust erodes sales and as online competitors deliver better-quality products cheaper and faster, it has become vital to develop engaging customer experiences. Customer journeys need to be smoother, richer, and more engaging – delivering consistent and positive experiences at every stage of the lifecycle, to maximise the chances of acquiring and retaining valued consumers.

As guardians of the customer journey, operations play a pivotal role reinforcing trust and loyalty in every transaction. As we've already discussed, customers expect faster and easier processes without a reduction in quality. They expect to be treated as valued users at every point and to enjoy seamless and smart experiences no matter which part of the organisation they're interacting with. They value honesty and transparency in all their interactions, especially when things go wrong.

Customers who are asked to repeat the same information at each contact point quickly disengage. Organisations that run contrasting or conflicting workflows (for example, between their retail and online stores) rapidly erode customer trust. Businesses that pass off customers to outsourced partners with different objectives or conflicting processes damage their brand.

Franchised organisations that don't effectively centralise customer data or coordinate consistent experiences frustrate customers who visit more than one store. Clients who are subject to drawn-out, bureaucratic, or inefficient processes will go elsewhere. Consumers who are given hollow excuses for product issues will tell everyone they know.

Operations are the frontline of capturing, storing, and protecting their customer's data. As data becomes more valuable and people become more sceptical, operations have a dramatically amplified responsibility to ensure that consumers continue to supply data, that it's used in the right ways, and that it's defended against growing cyber threats.

Facebook continues to struggle with operational data security after 50 million accounts were exposed in September 2018, which could result in a $1.63 billion fine.[7] Operational weaknesses exposed British Airways to a malicious criminal attack that affected 380,000 transactions, which could end up costing them a maximum of £489 million.[8]

Finally, operations have become a shop window for corporate ethics and social responsibility, playing a key role in addressing the demand for eco-friendly or sustainable production.

Walmart launched 'Project Gigaton' to radically change its operations and supply chain with the aim of reducing greenhouse-gas emissions by a gigaton by 2030.[9] Likewise, a coalition of investors and consumers forced BP, Mobil, Exxon, and Shell to reduce their carbon emissions and pollution in their production processes.[10]

Operations are vital to leverage the latest innovations

New technologies have opened up numerous opportunities. Operations has always been the key interface to extract greater value from technological advances. However, the sheer scale of what is now possible with data (both collection and analysis), platforms, materials, and zero marginal cost models dramatically amplifies operations' importance in connecting these innovations to value.

Operational teams and infrastructures are pivotal in enabling the latest technology to transform customer experiences. For example, powerful innovations such as augmented reality (AR) and virtual reality (VR) require operations to re-engineer existing customer journeys. Operations are required to rebuild key supply chain and manufacturing processes due to the potential of wearables and IoT in streamlining processes and reducing bottlenecks. They have to fundamentally redesign many of their processes and workflows due to the benefits of RPA in transforming back-office functions.

Operations are also critical to leverage the transformative power of data. The growth of open-source databases puts new demands on operational database systems. For years, database technology has converged around the relational database model, where enterprises would develop insights through consolidating proprietary data into one system. However, new models such as NoSQL, Big Data, and graph databases have opened up data sources and transformed the volume, velocity, and variety of data that companies can leverage. Operations are the linchpin in connecting their organisations to this potential value.

Finally, operations play a key role in connecting the old with the new. Game-changing initiatives have to work with existing infrastructures and processes. It's not enough to bolt on new capabilities to support mobile, cloud-based, device-infused customer experience applications if the existing systems and tools are unable to support them. Operations are essential in optimising legacy infrastructures and system interfaces to ensure that new technologies deliver their intended value.

More speed, less haste

In addition, organisations are increasingly dependent on operations reacting much quicker to mitigate the risk of competitive threats and capitalise on the benefits of market opportunities.

A faster-paced world demands faster reactions. Instant communication from customers and clients provides real-time feedback that has to be dealt with quickly and effectively. The right skills have to be deployed at the right time and in the right place to react to immediate threats. Innovations need to be integrated into operational workflows faster than ever. And the reaction to data security breaches must be quick, open, and efficient to mitigate the damage caused.

Operations are pivotal in effectively unifying external partners and specialists across their supply chain. As the demand for speed and experiences goes up while supply chains become more fragmented, operations are vital in connecting and streamlining all parts of the supply chain to deliver the intended results. As customers interact at more points on their journey, more data is captured, and opportunities come from anywhere – it's imperative that distributed supply chains operate as a single, cohesive unit.

Operations also play a more important role in quickly sharing intelligence. The power of data mining and advanced analytics depends on operational infrastructures effectively sharing significantly greater volumes of information across the supply chain. Operational systems and processes have to ensure that the right information is with the right function at the right time. This means guarding against content overload while ensuring that all relevant parts of the business are up to date with the latest developments.

Impact summary: Critical role

New operating realities are driving a significantly enhanced role for operational teams and infrastructures. Operational functions are increasingly a source of competitive advantage as they play a much more visible frontline role in interfacing with customers, optimising the latest technology, and reacting and adapting faster to change.

Optimising in the digital age

These impacts present a significant complication for many organisations. Over the past few decades, businesses have invested a lot of time, money, and resources into building operational teams and infrastructures that perform very specific tasks. Their role was to break workflows down into their constituent parts and drill down into tactical details to deliver incremental improvements.

Operational units focused inwards, becoming deeply entrenched in their part of the process rather than on the wider workflow. They concentrated their efforts on improving supply instead of adapting to changing demand – and measuring success through process efficiency instead of operational effectiveness. Technical infrastructures have evolved to monitor and control an exponential volume of tasks, which fragment as individual operating units target their particular operational risks.

However, this approach is less and less effective in the digital age. Customer experiences are inconsistent, strategic objectives are often misinterpreted, competitive threats go unchecked, and opportunities to deliver game-changing innovation are missed. As customer and workforce demand increases, systems and infrastructures built to deliver incremental efficiencies and compliance become stiff and cumbersome. As commercial complexity and operational risks increase, operational teams are now being forced to fundamentally rethink their approach.

Recommendation 13: Proactive simplification and risk allocation

Prioritise excellence over efficiency

Modern operations should shift their focus away from completing tasks to delivering strategic value. Instead of driving quantity outputs, they should switch to reinforcing quality outcomes. To this end, operational excellence has become a useful "management philosophy that goes beyond the traditional event-based model of improvement towards a longer-term change in culture".[11]

More than individual cost reduction and productivity improvement programmes, it approaches business and operational processes methodically and holistically, meeting customer expectations "through integrated performance across revenue, cost and risk". (ibid) Operational excellence balances operational demands with strategic imperatives, helping leaders to manage the tension between these occasionally contrasting drivers.

Start by **redefining and simplifying your definitions of operational value**. This helps your entire operational supply chain to focus on fewer, simpler operational objectives; reduces confusion, ambiguity and overlaps, while also helping to break down the silos between operating units. It also helps your operations move away from focusing on short-term task fulfilment to long-term value creation.

Some operational teams now target Customer Lifetime Value to ensure they focus as much on post-purchase interactions as pre-purchase. Many target customer advocacy to focus their teams on experiences instead of service. Others focus on the collective outputs of innovation, measuring the number of new products launched, patents acquired, or revenue from new products.

Next, **systematically update simplified definitions of value across the entire organisation**. A centralised methodical approach declutters the countless operational metrics that might have evolved within and between operating units and across owned and outsourced teams. Set a clear, consistent operational destination and demonstrate how following these new definitions will ensure that value flows to the customer. Focus on a small number of unambiguous objectives that clearly align to the intended strategy and guard against the fragmentation of operational goals and metrics.

Finally, make these new definitions **a cornerstone of the reformatted organisational culture** discussed in *Chapter 5: Culture*. Define, encourage, and reward the behaviours that focus on customer value. Constantly reinforce the importance of operational excellence over efficiency. Inspire commitment by giving operational teams ownership of customer value and freedom to proactively improve it.

Containerise

The simplification of operational elements into standardised components can dramatically reduce operational drag. Just like the advent of shipping containers greatly reduced the expense of international trade and increased its speed, the containerisation of operating resources allows actions to take place faster while simultaneously building in resilience and easier oversight. Containerisation can reduce frustrations by streamlining processes and systems, accelerate hand-offs between functional units, reduce risks by clarifying ownership, and create agility by removing ambiguity.

First, **define and standardise the 'containers' that form the key building blocks of your operation**. These might be the specific criteria for a handover between internal teams, standardised contracts and payment terms, definitions of objectives, or a clear allocation of risk for external partners. These templates not only clarify objectives and measures for each operating resource (defining costs and timescales), but also pre-qualify the specific inputs, outputs, and dependencies required before any transaction can take place.

For example, projects that require independent workers can be parcelled up into containers. Here, the definition of project success can be clearly defined, with agreed metrics supported by predefined legal documentation to manage expectations and risks. Inputs such as specific knowledge and experience – and outputs such as deadlines, formats and quality metrics are set out upfront. Essential information can be presented via an online platform to enable faster and more accurate identification, deployment, and fulfilment of the work.

Next, **develop systems and methods to ensure the efficient utilisation** of operational containers across the business. Significant savings can be made in opportunity costs if the movement of work along the supply chain is smooth or external resources can be brought in at the right time and hit the ground running. As not all work can always be delivered on plan, constantly tracking the performance of each container helps to proactively mitigate the risks. Here, resource management software can significantly enhance operational performance by planning projects, allocating existing resources, identifying gaps, and producing regular schedules.

Dynamic risk allocation

Operational excellence is a journey, not a destination. So, take an 'always on' approach to risk – continuously identifying risks and alternative solutions to mitigate any potential issues while proactively allocating liabilities as and when they occur.

Review and update your supplier contracts where possible. Although contracts should already align vision and clearly define roles, they can also clearly designate risk ownership, providing the clarity that underpins stronger, deeper relationships. On top of traditional requirements such as price, payment terms, and quality checks, contracts could also define unified measures of customer satisfaction, principles of communication, the way changes are accommodated, and how improvements and innovations can be incorporated. Pre-empting as many potential risks within the contract also helps to liberate operational leaders so they can spend more time on value creation.

Experiment with new supplier models. As operating landscapes become less predictable and uncertain, leaders should explore more flexible ways to manage their risk. 'As a service' approaches only charge for what is used in real time, rather than requiring long-term commitment to volumes or timescales.

Organisations get immediate access to specialist resources with reduced risk, as those resources can be scaled up or down according to actual demand. Costed in real time against specific profit and loss accounts (P&L), benefits can be measured against a dedicated project budget rather than generic corporate overheads. This helps to reduce gearing (the debt to equity ratio) on company books, as resources are paid out of operational rather than capital expenditure.

Finally, **build resilience and flexibility into operational supply chains**. Businesses are exposed if they keep all of their eggs in one supply basket. So, proactively develop relationships with multiple suppliers for each part of the supply chain to create operational flexibility, mitigate unforeseen risks, or ramp up additional capacity to exploit last-minute opportunities.

Be careful to qualify and quantify the potential costs and risks associated with multi-sourcing (for example, ensure that dual suppliers are not impacted by the same geographical or regulatory issues as the original partners) and continuously audit your risk exposure to get ahead of potential issues.

Recommendation summary: Proactive simplification and risk allocation

Increasing complexity requires a focus on simplicity. Operational teams should focus on proactive value creation, not reactive task completion, process efficiency, or cost reduction. In order to exploit fast-moving opportunities or defend against unexpected threats, they need to find ways to streamline their operational workflows. Systems, processes, and practices should enable greater agility and responsiveness across the business, continually allocating risks to better align liabilities to the strategy.

Recommendation 14: Focus on higher-value operational differentiators

Think about customer demand, not product supply

Focus on the outcome that your customers value, not the outputs your company delivers. Understand how customers interact with you now and how they want to interact in the future. Ensure that every customer journey gives consumers the experience they want, regardless of the channel they're using, building and reinforcing trust in every interaction.

Re-engineer processes around the customer journey, rather than organising them around existing functions. Assign dedicated resources to review and redesign each customer journey as it flows through the entire customer lifecycle. Within this, develop experience maps to identify the key hand-offs on different channels, the key assets that customers interact with, and the key points of weakness that need to be prioritised. Realign processes to that journey, updating and aligning assets while focusing on continuity and consistency.

Next, **proactively evaluate opportunities to enhance customer experiences** across the internal and outsourced supply chain. These interventions can be big or small. Chatbots can work much faster than traditional customer service teams, freeing up humans to focus on higher-value interventions. 3D printing can customise products to better meet customer expectations.

Recommendation engines like those at Amazon and Netflix use AI to deliver tailored product suggestions that enhance customers' lives.[12]

Differentiation can also come from much simpler improvements to existing processes, such as easier sign-up forms, phone consultations following a purchase, or personalised packaging.

Reconfigure operations to **constantly reinforce trust and loyalty throughout the customer lifecycle**. Most traditional operational processes assume that customer trust is a constant, and they work on the basis that once it has been won, it cannot be lost. As a result, trust and reputation tend to get ignored in post-purchase operational workflows.

Instead, update all customer processes to make them easy, open, and transparent. Change your processes to end customer harassment for repeat business. Double-down your efforts to improve data security throughout the customer lifecycle, reinforcing how data is securely captured, used, and stored, and importantly, what it won't be used for. Include customer lifetime value or net promoter scores (NPS) in post-purchase operational performance metrics.

Measure and reward operational excellence as well as efficiency

Although the operational elements of customer experience, organisational agility, effective innovation, access to critical resources, and culture are vital to commercial success, they are rarely included in the operational analysis, budgets, and risks measures of today. Instead, redevelop your operational metrics, incorporating these new values while updating how they are quantified, incentivising distributed operational teams to deliver against them.

Accurately **define the measures that support your simplified operational values**. Assuming that you have defined new measures of operational value, develop metrics that accurately evaluate the intended goal. Reducing the frequency of bug fixes or above-average CSAT scores might achieve a transactional target, but this does not address a key differentiator of long-term customer experience.

Some organisations have introduced customer lifetime value to measure how much revenue they can expect one customer to generate over the course of the relationship. Others use NPS to measure overall customer advocacy (rather than CSAT, which measures reactions to single events), enabling businesses to identify strengths and weaknesses across their supply chain.

Incentivise operational leaders and teams more on proactive risk mitigation and less on reactive fault-fixing. This encourages operational decision-makers to make great tactical decisions to solve customer problems in real time. Reward individuals for listening, being honest with customers, and owning problems rather than how efficiently they apply standardised processes. Measure the flow of information within your business and incentivise the sharing of operational intelligence between and within functions.

Apply these measures and rewards to both external partners and internal employees. If you only evaluate a supplier on transactional task-completion (such as compliance or timeliness) when the rest of the supply chain is focused on customer experience or innovation, it will undermine overall operational performance. Linking supplier rewards to core operational values and tactical customer experiences helps to align all parts of the supply chain to achieve common goals.

Better leverage a symbiotic partner network

In the digital age, companies are gaining access to far more creativity, thought leadership, commercial collaboration, competitive intelligence, and technology via their growing ecosystem of partners, suppliers, independent workers, and research organisations. This extended workforce helps to manage risks, exploit opportunities, and provide new opportunities to create value. Investing in stronger, collaborative, and constructive partner relationships helps businesses to capitalise on this vital network.

Start by **updating the criteria to select and engage external partners and suppliers**. External providers shouldn't be selected exclusively on cost, but on values and purpose alignment (as well as effective allocation and transparency of risks, as covered in the previous section). Evaluate how well partners can align their businesses to updated customer journeys and reinforce a consistent customer experience. Measure how well suppliers align to your organisational values and culture to improve collaboration and protect company reputation.

Spend more time developing constructive supplier relationships. Game-changing innovations and solutions increasingly come from external experts with deeper, stronger knowledge and more recent exposure to the latest technology and thinking. Invest in key supplier relationships to build loyalty and commitment.

Try embedding key employees with partners to improve communications, align values, and focus on your customers' experiences. Engage more often and closely with external supplier communities, providing information and forums to build mutual understanding and relationships, while simultaneously spreading supply risk. Some businesses even leverage communications platforms to capture supplier feedback and suggestions on both operational and strategic improvements.

Finally, **develop new supplier collaborations** to capitalise on fast-moving opportunities. New methods of creating value are developing through distributed partner networks. Innovative solutions are delivered by uniting different entities to develop new concepts or leverage existing assets differently to deliver ground-breaking solutions. Try proactively networking with different organisations, both inside and outside your existing communities. Allocate a budget to prototype and market test new ideas with like-minded organisations, identifying new opportunities to create customer value.

Recommendation summary: Higher-value operational differentiators

Operational success is built on the differentiators that stakeholders value the most. Organisations can no longer wring consistent savings out of unstable prices or diversify production quickly enough to meet changing demands if they are wedded to incremental efficiency. Instead, businesses must recalibrate their operational engines to focus on customer demand, not product supply, investing in and rewarding constructive, collaborative relationships, and operational excellence with their on-demand partners.

Recommendation 15: Invest in an empowered infrastructure

Leverage the old with the new

Digital operations can increase speed to market, make employees more productive, promote leaner processes, and maximise asset utilisation. But becoming a digital business means applying technology to enable completely new types of products and processes, rather than simply enhancing existing processes and modes of interaction.[13] Now, organisations have to proactively identify the new technologies that can deliver revolutionary operational improvements.

However, years of focusing on cost savings and efficiency have rendered many legacy systems unable to support faster business cycle times. Data is often trapped, and incumbent systems, processes, and tools are inflexible and cumbersome, struggling to keep up. It's not enough to buy and bolt on new technology to succeed. Organisations need to ensure that any new technology is integrated with an effective core enterprise system that empowers success.

First, **evaluate how well your core enterprise systems can support new game-changing technologies**. Legacy systems often complicate digital operational capability, but replacing them isn't always a choice. Find ways to turn your existing infrastructures into a strength that can be leveraged, rather than a burden that restricts. Explore your current functionality to see how it can be improved, while investigating how the software can be reconfigured to support crucial new technology and/or work with software providers to develop and launch essential improvements.

If after this, your current enterprise system still cannot support key technology, **investigate viable data integration platforms** to plug the gap. Overlaying a next-generation platform on a legacy system allows businesses the freedom to leverage new, more cost-efficient, open-source solutions for newly developed applications while retaining the robust functional capabilities of their traditional infrastructure. Here, service layers act as middleware between legacy systems and applications. Data access layers abstract the data, allowing simplified access to multiple data stores. And application program interfaces (APIs) expose the functions of the legacy system to outside development and improvement.[14]

Finally, ensure your upgraded technology infrastructure **prioritises the protection of customers' data at all costs**. Ensure customer data is securely stored and robust defensive safeguards are put in place to guard against external threats. Focus on internal weaknesses, such as thumb drives or the use of personal file hosting services, and train all human capital to spot, prevent or mitigate data-security risks. Regularly audit your organisation's ability to protect customer information, simulating data-loss scenarios to test workforce alertness and reaction times.

Get ahead of the curve

Although not everything within an operational environment requires updating, there are workflows or segments of a process that are pivotal to an organisation's success. Operational teams have to get ahead of demand, constantly evolving and testing new solutions to deliver trailblazing improvements. However, evolving these new activities cannot be done in a 'live' operational environment – to do so dangerously undermines current operational capability.

Instead, try developing a parallel operational approach where solutions can be explored, tested, and prototyped before being launched. This approach can vary in size according to demand and risk, but should be ring-fenced from the main operational business to ensure that explorations capture empirical evidence without undermining existing activity.

Try **appointing a person or team as a focal point for any experimentation**. This 'exploration team' can clearly articulate the ambition for any operational improvements and define the specific demands, goals, and criteria that any potential solutions are assessed against. Acting as a guide, they ensure that suggestions are thoroughly qualified, testing criteria are robust and meaningful, and any prototyping is fully aligned to the organisation's strategic objectives.

Crucially, their evaluation criteria must be aligned to new definitions of operational value and success, rather than the old tactical metrics.

This exploration team can **leverage collaboration and internal crowdsourcing** as a method to drive innovation. Operational teams can be encouraged and incentivised to focus on the critical steps and processes that the exploration team has identified, through empirical analysis, as the most impactful. Exploration teams can create feedback loops between them and the operational frontline, encouraging problem-solving at a localised as well as a more strategic level.

Finally, organisations ought to consider a **range of exploration approaches and platforms**. For example, specialist software such as Proto.io or Axure offer scalable options to mock up, test, and develop technical prototypes.[15] Try partnering with universities that offer advanced research facilities, testing capabilities, and teams to evolve solutions. At the more holistic end of the spectrum, organisations can partner with specialist innovation companies to transform entire parts of their business operations engine.

Enable responsiveness

Infrastructures shouldn't replace humans, but should liberate them to make higher-value interventions, "reacting quickly and effectively to a wide range of business events as they occur".[16] Configure systems to empower organisational alertness, proactively mitigating risks before they manifest as operational issues. Dynamically modify operational workflows in response to changing customer demands to support new products and services. Share data and insights effectively across extended operational teams to enable better and faster decisions.

Some organisations are already implementing **proactive monitoring to identify issues and contact customers in advance** of problems.

> According to Ben Kerschberg, CEO of BKC3 Consulting Group, some businesses are offering new IoT services that alert a company on the failure of its product in advance of the customer contacting the company or even noticing the fault. Real-time data analysis triggers a "proactive visit from a service person, a part is replaced before it fails and services are scheduled by the customer at a time that works for them".[17]

As customer expectations drive new products and services, operations should **regularly adapt the roles that support new offerings**. Continuously learn from your customers, updating role responsibilities and experiences required to better align to customer requirements. By leveraging the exploration team's parallel approach, operations can iteratively improve and evolve roles and responsibilities *before* launching new offerings, deploying existing or new human capital depending on demand.

Effectively and securely share customer data across the entire supply chain to enable quicker decision-making based on real-time insights. Triangulate insights from multiple sources to reconnect decision-makers with customers and enable different parts of the organisation to respond faster and/or collaborate better. Data and insights from partners and suppliers can also be shared, creating a virtuous cycle of reciprocal intelligence across the supply chain.

Recommendation summary: Empowered infrastructures

Embrace digital technology, balancing essential investment in existing infrastructures with critical innovations that deliver competitive advantage. Get ahead of demand, testing and refining key operational processes to deliver competitive advantage. Enable improved responsiveness to react faster and better to a wider range of operational events and demands.

Operational Excellence

IMPACT OF FORCES

I13. *Growing pressure on operational functions*	**I14.** *Changed operational realities*	**I15.** *Increasingly critical role delivering The Plan*
Everyday business activities changing more regularly • Support wider range of faster moving products and services • External forces demand more regular course corrections • Changing customer relationships	**Focussing on production efficiency increases exposure** • Teams deflected • Declining differentiation • Less prepared for new threats	**Critical to positive customer experience** • Pivotal to reinforcing trust and loyalty in every transaction • Frontline of capturing, storing and protecting customer data • Shop window for corporate ethics and social value
Increased operational complexity • Demand more tailored products and experiences • More fragmented supply chain • Manage and monitor expanded contractual requirements	**Permanent workforce less agile and cost-effective** • Accelerating markets demand new skills that change more often • Skills relevant and valuable for less time • Traditional talent supply cannot keep up	**Vital interface to leverage latest innovations** • Enable latest technology to transform experiences • Leverage transformative power of metadata • Connect old infrastructures with new capabilities
Greater operational risk • Significant opex, capex and liabilities inflate risk • Operational costs harder to forecast and control • Diminishing returns from incumbent infrastructures	**Uneven playing surface** • Different risk and liability profiles of new competitors • Challengers come from anywhere • Operating rules don't apply consistently	**More speed, less haste** • Faster-paced world demands faster reactions • Unify fragmented and distributed supply chain • Key to sharing intelligence

RECOMMENDATIONS — ACTIVATE

R13. *Proactive simplification and risk allocation*	**R14.** *Focus on higher-value operational differentiators*	**R15.** *Invest in empowered infrastructure*
Prioritise excellence over efficiency • Redefine and simplify definitions of operational value • Apply consistently across organisation • Make cornerstone of culture	**Focus on customer demand, not product supply** • Re-engineer processes around customer journey • Evaluate opportunities to enhance experiences • Constantly reinforce trust and loyalty throughout customer lifecycle	**Leverage old with new** • Evaluate current software capability • Investigate viable data integration platform • Prioritise protection of customer data
Containerise • Define and standardise key 'containers' • Develop systems and methods to ensure efficient utilisation	**Measure and reward excellence as well as efficiency** • Define new measures of operational value • Incentivise proactive risk mitigation, not reactive fault-fixing • Apply consistently to whole supply chain	**Get ahead of the curve** • Appoint exploration team • Crowdsource innovation • Experiment with different approaches and platforms
Dynamic risk allocation • Review and update supplier contracts • Experiment with new supplier models • Build resilience and flexibility into supply chains	**Better leverage symbiotic network** • Update partnership criteria • Invest in constructive supplier relationships • Develop new collaborations	**Enable responsiveness** • Invest in proactive monitoring and response • Regularly adapt roles to support new offerings • Effectively and securely share customer data

CHAPTER 9

Leveraging Human Capital

Human capital is defined as "the knowledge, skills, competencies and other attributes embodied in individuals or groups of individuals acquired during their life and used to produce goods, services or ideas in market circumstance".[1] Organisations seek to exploit these human attributes to gain competitive advantage.

Human capital management (HCM) is an approach taken by many organisations to effectively manage workers, and is traditionally delivered by Human Resource (HR) functions who strive to maximise human performance through a mix of strategic and tactical initiatives. These range from talent acquisition (TA) and learning and development (L&D) to organisational change and industrial relations. In larger organisations, specialist teams are responsible for carrying out these initiatives.

HR has played an important role within organisations for over 150 years. An output of the second industrial revolution, companies sought ways to better manage their human capital as more and more workers moved into cities and factories. With the human relations movement of the early 20th century, the discipline evolved to address the social needs of workers, eliciting their cooperation to create business value.

As organisations got bigger and more complex, so did the hierarchies and operational infrastructures required to manage them. Personnel functions grew to help administer this complexity, supplementing their welfare role to include payroll and benefits, hiring, and health and safety. In these increasingly paternalistic organisations defined by 'command and control', Personnel's role was to centralise and administer the numerous processes that had developed, reduce operational 'people costs' through economies of scale, and support management in their interactions with employees – either as individuals or via trade unions. The value of Personnel was predominantly characterised by transactional service and administrative efficiency.

In the last few decades of the 20th century, Personnel matured into Human Resources, reflecting a move towards a more integrated and commercially focused function. HR updated its purpose – supplementing its administration and service role with more proactive and commercially driven interventions.

Today, many HR functions continue to explore new ways to increase the value they deliver, and increasing numbers of HR leaders occupy roles on boards of directors or within executive leadership teams.

Why should leaders care?

People represent the greatest asset to organisations. In his book *The Fourth Industrial Revolution* (Portfolio Penguin, 2016), Klaus Schwab (founder and executive chairman of the World Economic Forum) stated that "talent, more than capital, will represent the critical production factor. For this reason, scarcity of a skilled workforce rather than the availability of financial capital is more likely to be the crippling limit to innovation, competitiveness and growth."

By these same measures, people are also an organisation's greatest risk. They are one of the largest fixed costs on the balance sheet, yet their productivity cannot be guaranteed or precisely controlled. Disengaged human capital can dramatically restrict performance, innovation, and customer experience, while a shortage of appropriate or engaged talent can limit or prevent organisations from capitalising on opportunities or defending against threats.

Human capital, HCM, and HR have become critical management levers in the digital age. Executives have never held a more important role in setting the right people agenda. Operational leaders have never played a more crucial part in extracting people value. And the HR function has never been in a better place to transform the fortunes of business.

Impact of the forces

Many established HR approaches are struggling to keep up with changing demand. A focus on rules, compliance, and administrative standardisation restricts an organisation's ability to quickly adapt to rapidly evolving circumstances. Deep-seated expectations of HR service and support undermine the power of culture and updated leadership methods. Traditional talent supply approaches are not configured to deliver the behaviours and skills that deliver competitive advantage at the speed required. Legacy HR infrastructures are unable to cope with fundamentally different operating realities. The digital world is asking very different questions that traditional HR is struggling to answer.

Impact 16: People value has to be extracted faster, more dynamically, and more cost-effectively

Compressed timescales

Organisations now have far less time to extract value from their human capital. As product lifecycles decrease and new competitors disrupt markets, windows of opportunity are compressed and new threats appear more often. Each function within HR is under increased pressure to deliver better outcomes – and faster.

Leaders and their HR partners have less time to galvanise their teams and functions to hit faster-moving targets. There is less time to unite more diverse, distributed, and demanding workforces or deliver more fluid and demanding goals. Operational HR has less time to process day-to-day people transactions, mitigate operational people issues, and respond to more requests and tactical challenges.

TA teams have to find, acquire, and deploy the right talent quicker than ever. They need to discover, connect, and exploit distributed talent pools, quickly building stronger candidate relationships while assessing candidate suitability earlier in their process. They have to race against increased competition, accelerating their hiring processes without compromising quality and onboarding talent faster to meet accelerating demand.

L&D teams have less time to upskill employees, delivering learning in what McKinsey termed "learning at the speed of business".[2] They have to evolve newer capabilities faster, while constantly realigning training interventions to meet changing commercial priorities. And they have to provide access to a greater range of learning opportunities so teams are more prepared to respond to fast-changing commercial environments.

Large permanent workforces carry more risk

As discussed in *Chapter 6: Structure and Leadership*, for many businesses, employee reward (pay and benefits) and physical real estate are the most significant components of their fixed operating costs. However, as established operating models are disrupted and economic foundations weaken, large fixed people costs increase an organisation's operational hazards and liabilities. Many businesses are now reconsidering their long-held views on 'owning' workforces and workplaces in favour of new, dynamic ways to manage their people costs.

Balance sheet liabilities are inflated by large permanent workforces that carry significant fixed payroll costs and corresponding health and pension commitments. Extensive provisions in full-time employment contracts, such as extended notice periods, can limit an organisation's financial flexibility, while larger infrastructures are required to support larger permanent workforces, further adding to operational expenditure. All of these additional provisions impact cashflow, restricting an organisation's ability to invest in opportunities or defend against threats.

In addition, the large real estate required to house an 'owned' workforce inflates costs and risks. As workforces become more distributed, cloud-based infrastructures virtualise back-office functions, and collaboration software improves remote productivity – owned real estate is increasingly underutilised, creating unnecessary liabilities. As the size, shape, and location of the workforce changes more regularly, long-term commitments to large real estate carry more risk. As a result, many organisations are considering fundamentally different workspace approaches, either by reconfiguring their existing space for better use or finding ways to reduce their physical footprint.

Agile businesses require agile workforces and people processes

Faster-moving markets require faster-moving workforces. HR processes, policies, systems, and infrastructures now have to enable greater speed and agility. They have to reduce barriers to execution without compromising their effectiveness, while also enabling distributed workforces to collaborate faster and make better decisions together to optimise productivity.

However, many HR approaches were designed to deliver compliance rather than productivity. Prescriptive people processes prioritise risk management over speed, often increasing the number and complexity of steps that human capital needs to follow in the performance of their everyday duties. Reactive HR service workflows mean that time is lost waiting to respond to challenges, rather than proactively mitigating potential issues. HR systems and communication platforms geared exclusively to serve permanent full-time employees limit critical information-sharing across distributed teams.

The impact of these traditional HR approaches creates organisational drag. Indeed, there is a negative impact on productivity as increased demand has to navigate rigid and complicated HR processes, systems, and infrastructures.

A 2015 study by the Economist Intelligence Unit (commissioned by Bain) surveyed 300 companies across the globe with $500 million+ revenues to quantify the impact of HCM on productivity.[3] They found that the average company loses 25% of its productive capacity to drag from HR processes.

Impact summary: Extract people value

Political and economic uncertainty, rapidly evolving technology, demanding shareholders, and exacting customers create a business environment where people value has to be extracted quicker than ever. As new economic approaches disrupt established operating models and access to global investment falls, large owned workforces and workspaces reduce financial flexibility and increase operational risk. People and processes need to become more agile to capitalise on faster-moving opportunities and defend against faster-moving threats. Unfortunately, many existing HR approaches seem to do the opposite, creating organisational drag that slows businesses down.

Impact 17: The changing value of human capital and human capital management (HCM)

People are an increasing source of competitive advantage

These days, customers trust people, not products. While the mantra 'people buy from people' is perhaps too generic (if that were true, why the exponential growth in Amazon?)[4], the workforce plays an enhanced role in creating trust and credibility. Consumers are sceptical of organisations that only push their latest products and instead look for personal connections that reliably advise them on what they need. Clients are less interested in individual product features and costs and more interested in commercial collaborations that continually add value. In a world where stakeholder expectations are shifting, consumers are buying from people they trust.

In this world, human capital plays a much more important role. Human capital delivers greater customer loyalty, improves sales through distributed recommendations, and enriches corporate reputations. Employees positively differentiate products and services from competitor offerings that are cheaper or easier to buy elsewhere. Skilled talent delivers personalised experiences that engage customers, allowing organisations to command higher prices as customers and clients perceive greater value in the relationship. And with the explosion of social media and instant communication platforms that bypass corporate marketing controls, entire workforces play a role in customer relations.

Talent also plays an enhanced role in developing new products and services, creating better customer experiences, or developing new processes and systems that deliver game-changing results. Innovation is no longer restricted to a few individuals, certain times, or specialist research and development departments, but is instead dispersed throughout organisations. Business are reliant on a much greater proportion of their human capital differentiating their offerings throughout the customer lifecycle, better meeting customer needs, saving costs, improving margins and creating valuable intellectual property (IP).

Changing skills demand and the expanding skills gap

Commercial success is increasingly dependent on a different set of skills and behaviours. Markets are evolving so quickly that the "half-life of skills is rapidly falling".[5] AI, automation, and other technologies are replacing the transactional skills required in regular, repeatable work, while subject matter expertise is available on demand from a growing independent workforce and specialist partners. Businesses are increasingly reliant on the cognitive skills and behaviours that can unravel complex issues, solve dynamic problems in real time, and enable distributed collaboration.

Critical reasoning and entrepreneurial skills are now vital workforce attributes required to spot and grow new economic opportunities. The ability to interrogate multiple, unconnected data sources, decipher insights, and make quick, accurate, and balanced decisions are essential leadership qualities. Effective collaboration, teamwork, and empathy across the entire supply chain underpins an organisation's ability to effectively develop and apply solutions to urgent challenges.

The demand for 'digital literacy' is also growing rapidly. As society develops new and deeper relationships and dependencies with machines in the workplace and at home, the nature of the human-machine work partnership is evolving.[6] As new technology comes and goes and consumer expectations of constant relevance grow, meeting their increasing demands requires ever-improving digital knowledge and capability. Data security is no longer an IT problem but a business problem – requiring risk mitigation strategies across every part of the workforce. Human capital increasingly has to combine critical thinking and social skills with the ability to apply technical solutions to societal and commercial requirements.

However, many traditional talent supply approaches are unable to keep up with these changing demands, exposing businesses to a growing shortage of critical competencies. Many TA functions continue to screen candidates solely on transactional skills or previous experience, inadvertently selecting out the highest-value behaviours. L&D functions focused on generic batch-training programmes are unable to deliver the volume or diversity of competencies needed at the speed required. Supply-chain relationships that do not require outsourced partners to contribute the same essential attributes with their host company risk compromising the productivity and profitability of their extended workforce.

Changing leader expectations

As demand for organisations to extract greater value from their workforces in shorter timescales increases, the definition of HR value is moving away from reactive service, administration, and support towards a more proactive, commercially-driven leadership role.

Senior leaders already understand the importance of a more commercial HR function in delivering the strategy. While they expect HR basics to be done efficiently and effectively, they also require HR to enable the business to make people decisions that deliver better commercial returns. HR value is increasingly defined not by service and support but by ensuring that the business has the right skills, competencies, and attributes in the right place and time to optimise commercial opportunities.

As a result, many leaders are changing their expectations of HR.

In his research paper *What CEOs Want from HR* (Henley Business School, 2014), Professor Nick Holley discovered that 41% of CEOs think their HR heads are "too focused on process and rules" and 37% think HR doesn't "understand the business well enough".[7] McKinsey research supports this, with a July 2017 quarterly article suggesting that CEOs should accelerate the reinvention of HR.[8]

With their growing enlightenment, many senior leaders expect very different outcomes from their HR functions. They want HR to play a key business role, not just a functional one, helping to deliver commercial results, not just services and support. They understand the power of people and culture, and they expect HR teams to lead the efforts to unlock potential in the workforce. In an increasingly interconnected world, the value of HR is being fundamentally redefined.

Impact summary: Changing value

The definition of human capital value is changing, as talent plays a much bigger role in building customer trust, differentiating products and services, and improving loyalty. People are a critical source of profitability, which in turn is driving greater demand for new behavioural competencies that deliver competitive advantage. This is having a profound impact on HCM and HR, challenging them to move away from a traditional, reactive service approach towards a more proactive, commercial leadership role.

Impact 18: Changing HR operating realities

Changing talent motivations

The balance of employment power is shifting, as workers seek greater autonomy and alignment with the companies they work for. According to Deloitte's report 'The rise of the social enterprise', organisations today "are increasingly judged on the basis of their relationships with their workers, their customers, and their communities, as well as their impact on society at large".[9] Organisational reputations are increasingly visible and more important to demanding talent.

At the same time, human capital is changing in nature – shifting from a passive resource to an active asset. Skilled, talented workers no longer look for set jobs, but instead for mutually beneficial working partnerships that empower their long-term careers. They are attracted to organisations that reflect their values and beliefs, rather than ones that expect them to assimilate. They expect more personalised and holistic rewards – including fair and open pay, while looking for expanded benefits that promote their wellbeing.

Proactively managing organisational reputation has therefore become critical. As information about organisations and their leaders becomes readily available, rated, and more actively shared, businesses can no longer leave their reputation to chance. HR now has to shape perceptions across a greater volume of channels and in more markets to position themselves effectively with demanding talent.

As perceptions are increasingly influenced by all the interactions that talent has with a business, reputation management has to ensure that those values and behaviours are consistently and congruently reflected across their entire talent lifecycle. For example, recruiters can no longer leave candidates to sit in the black hole of their Applicant Tracking System (ATS) without a timely personalised response, and core HR cannot ignore negative behaviours from workers in any part of their distributed workforce.

Finally, as working lives extend significantly in length and the half-life of skills falls, talent has started to prioritise opportunities for personal development. Talent is now far more proactive, hunting new experiences rather than reactively waiting for potential promotions. As technology gives workers better access to career and learning opportunities, they are less reliant on line managers or traditional career models to tell them what to do, operating outside traditional vertical succession plans.

Glassdoor data reveals that among millennials, the "ability to learn and progress" is now the principal driver of a company's employment brand. Yet only one-third of millennials believe that their organisation is using their skills well, and 42% say they are likely to leave because they are not learning fast enough.[10] Mark Spelman of the World Economic Forum argues that the ability to keep the top 30% of talent will depend on long-term corporate training.[11]

Growing complexity

Workforces are increasingly diverse, distributed, and discerning. A greater proportion of the workforce is starting to operate outside standard permanent employment relationships. Globally distributed teams and evolving workplace models mean that fewer teams are co-located under one roof. As more employees pursue non-linear career paths and personal career agendas, HR has to find new ways to deal with significantly increased complexity.

HR now has to find ways to unify multi-generational, multi-cultural, multi-location teams to focus on specific outputs. They need to encourage and embed the right behaviours while proactively dealing with the wrong ones, effectively blending permanent, independent, and outsourced parts of the supply chain to operate productively and efficiently.

Traditional attraction channels such as print advertising are less effective as candidates disengage from the established top-down, unilateral 'push' marketing approaches established in many recruitment departments. In fact, candidate behaviour now closely matches the changing customer behaviours discussed at length in *Chapter 7: Positioning for Success*. Talent has moved online to access 'independent' information on potential employers via indirect channels, third parties, and peer-to-peer platforms, moving away from job boards and company websites.

At the same time, personalised, immediate, and valuable experiences have become the expectation in the world of work. Just as consumers expect better experiences throughout the customer lifespan, talent now expects better experiences at every stage of the talent lifecycle, whether this is employees, candidates, or independent workers. They also seek relevant, compelling, and trustworthy content, delivered in the appropriate context to ensure impact.

Increased transactional demand

Far more human capital will start to flow through organisations. As TA connects to more diverse networks in more distributed locations, the volume of candidate traffic will grow. As talent is increasingly hired onto projects instead of roles, the volume of new starters and leavers will escalate. As more independent human capital flows in, through, and out of the business, HR functions will have to find new ways to track and manage their movement.

As internal 'liquid' workforces travel across organisations in more fluid, dynamic ways, HR functions have to enable more multi-directional movement, accurately tracking a more extensive range of human capital attributes and matching them more often to a broader, faster-moving range of opportunities. As talent pursues multi-stage careers, HR has to facilitate a greater range of career pathways across traditional hierarchical boundaries.

HR also has to be increasingly responsive, reacting quicker and more effectively to external and internal requests. As the demand for continuous learning increases, L&D teams have to increase the breadth and depth of their learning offering while connecting a much larger volume of workers to a greater number of learning providers. TA teams must proactively monitor a much larger range of channels, responding appropriately and quickly to a wider range of requests.

Impact summary: Operational realities

HR now plays a significantly enhanced operational role to effectively leverage human capital. TA teams now have to connect with more diverse platforms and networks to access critical pools of talent, engaging them via new strategies to 'pull' human capital towards them. Core HR has to support huge increases in transactional workflows as candidates, employees, and independent workers move into the business, through it, then out of it in greater volumes. All HR needs to motivate and integrate a greater volume, range, and diversity of talent while L&D has to provide better access to a greater range of learning opportunities to keep talent engaged and productive.

Optimising in the digital age

Despite all of these impacts, many businesses continue to leverage their existing HR approaches. Many continue to 'own' predominantly permanent workforces working set hours in large, expensive, and under-utilised buildings. Lots still have convoluted multi-layer hierarchies commanding and controlling the workforce from the top down. Countless organisations still follow multiple, centralised, heavily prescriptive people processes that leverage large, complicated labour-intensive infrastructures. Yet these approaches are being exposed as too slow, risky, rigid, bureaucratic, and cumbersome to deliver competitive advantage in the digital age.

So how can businesses adapt their approach to human capital in the digital age? How can they refocus on higher-value people interventions without dropping the ball on the basics?

Recommendation 16: Speed to value, not speed to service

Entrepreneurial HR

HR have to start thinking and acting as business leaders, not business partners. To design and deliver the people interventions that have the greatest returns, HR functions have to understand their organisation's constantly evolving commercial environment and be clear on the drivers of competitive advantage and risk. Crucially, they have to be credible and trusted by the rest of the business to ensure they have impact.

Any HR function has to first understand what drives the value of their business. Instead of focusing on transactional efficiency or rules and regulations, target your HR function to understand what makes your business successful.

> Sandy Ogg (former CHRO of Unilever and founder of CEO.works) discovered this fundamental principle when he stepped into private equity (PE). Ogg noticed that two things had to be right for PE in every investment. One: buy the right asset at the right price, and two: have "enough of the right people to create value in a compressed timeframe". For PE, HR's role was to connect talent to value quickly in order to create organisational speed.[12]

That means no matter how big or small the function, **HR has to first think like an investor**, to stop looking 'inside out' and start looking 'outside in'. According to Professor Dominic Swords (Business Economist at Henley Business School), HR functions have to first define clear and simple measures of shareholder value.[13] These value measures help HR to understand why an investor should start and continue to invest in their organisation, from how value is calculated to which variables are used to assess proposals.

Next, HR should **identify areas of value creation and value at risk**, understanding how their specialism can positively impact them. For example, instead of TA prioritising transactional metrics like 'time to fill' or 'cost per hire', they can focus on identifying and acquiring the critical behaviours and skills that deliver customer value faster than the competition. Subsequent HR actions can be prioritised based on their importance to creating or defending value, rather than urgency or noise, keeping the business focused on the human capital interventions that deliver the overall plan.

To effectively deliver these new targets, **HR must build their commercial credibility**. Swords recommends that HR evolves the capability to engage in dialogue with executives on their terms, as well as developing a comprehensive understanding of changing customer demands and the shifting competitor landscape. HR practitioners should build their business reasoning and analytical skills to turn the wealth of new data and information into valuable insights and judgements. They should spend far more time outside HR to immerse themselves in business issues and industry challenges, while also building the knowledge, networks, behaviours, and skills required to run a business.

Reposition HR

As people become the key factor in production, HR plays one of the most important roles in any organisation. Unfortunately, their potential to deliver enhanced outcomes is often significantly limited by an organisation-wide perception of HR as a support function. The legacy of Taylorian production efficiency and management's strong expectations of service and administration restrict HR's capacity to deliver higher-value strategic interventions. Previous attempts by HR to be strategic have left them overstretched, leading to a self-fulfilling vicious cycle of underperformance and underinvestment.

Senior leaders have to break this cycle by **confronting the legacy barriers that have restricted previous efforts**. Don't tolerate the well-worn mantras from some in your management teams (and indeed some senior HR people) that HR is about service. Instead, invest in HR leadership that understands the changing reality, is deeply commercial (or has the potential to be), and is primarily focused on company, rather than functional performance.

Lead the communications to reposition HR throughout your organisation and invest time, resources, and budget to empower an HR strategy and team that creates stakeholder value. Update the measures of HR value, proactively sharing those across the business so that everyone understands HR's evolving role.

For their part, **line managers must reassume responsibility** for many of the people practices that they've previously passed back to HR. While automation and improved enterprise software are already making many repeatable and transactional HR tasks easier to complete, line managers have to take clear ownership of people management. Hold line managers accountable for their people decisions and motivate them to develop the organisation's leadership, and urge employees to solve problems directly with their leaders. The management of people is the responsibility of people managers, not HR!

Finally, empower HR to **redefine the HR behaviours and skills required for the digital age**. Encourage them to let go of old definitions of service and administration and embrace the commercial competencies required of true business leaders. Ask them to redesign their roles around the creation of commercial value and the management of strategic risk. Ensure that strong financial and analytical acumen accompany intellectual versatility, customer-centricity, creativity, and digital literacy. HR should also develop specific HR metrics that measure value creation, tying HR performance back to the strategy.

Proactively reduce operational HR drag

Lead your HR function to move beyond enforcing rules, regulations, and policies to instead address the barriers that stifle speed and creativity. Incentivise HR to find ways to cut through bureaucratic density, compressing processes without reducing their overall effectiveness.

HR functions should go through their policies, procedures, rules, and regulations and challenge themselves to **remove any steps that don't deliver defined benefits**. This means stripping back processes to their shortest and simplest effective state to increase speed of execution and the chances of adoption. This could mean replacing centralised performance evaluations with less formalised check-in processes as Adobe did[14], not tracking employee holidays, or not demanding receipts for low-cost items in the expenses process. Importantly, HR cannot assume automation will do this for them, as automating convoluted processes doesn't necessarily stop them from being convoluted.

Encourage HR to *proactively* **apply people processes** wherever possible. Onboarding and induction processes can be delivered remotely and on demand before an employee's start date to shorten the time to productivity. Depending on hiring profiles and volumes, rolling interview cycles can maintain a constant flow of qualified talent without waiting for headcount accounting processes to trigger individual recruitment campaigns. Security and reference-checking can be initiated earlier in the hiring process, leveraging the latest technology to reduce delays to new starters.

Finally, HR has to proactively **reduce the legacy barriers to engaging independent workers**. As independent workers play a greater role in delivering customer experiences and innovation, HR has to reposition their value to the business while making it easier for managers to leverage this critical resource. For example, HR could start to 'containerise' independent worker roles to deliver absolute clarity on inputs and outputs, clearly defining the measures of success as well as duration and costs. Or they could access 'smart contracts', which use blockchain technology so workers don't have to be uploaded to payroll or individually administered through centralised finance systems.[15]

Recommendation summary: Speed to value

In today's economy, human capital value comes from an agile, adaptable, engaged, highly capable workforce that can be dynamically flexed in response to shifting global forces. HR's purpose is to ensure that the right people are in the right place at the right time and at the right cost, with the right engagement to deliver the right results. Instead of focusing on speed to service, HR needs to reconfigure around *speed to value*, maximising the business's chances of commercial success while proactively mitigating challenges.

This means that HR can no longer focus on trying to juice incremental efficiencies out of their existing approaches. Doing more of the same will no longer deliver competitive advantage. Empowered by the whole business, HR has to move away from a function-centric role partnering on processes to a business-centric role leading commercial results.

Recommendation 17: Get ahead of the curve

Build next-generation workforce planning

As the half-life of skills plummets and demand for different behaviours grows, organisations have to more accurately predict the critical knowledge and competencies that deliver competitive advantage. To improve the management of costs and risks, businesses have to be much better at defining when, where, and how long these new competencies are required for. To quickly and accurately connect supply to demand, organisations need to effectively track and coordinate their entire distributed workforce.

First, **invest in a continuously updated strategic workforce plan**. A 'living' plan, regularly updated with real data, moves beyond the annual budget cycle that sets cost/headcount limits and reports on fixed roles. Instead, it dynamically links supply to demand, forecasting how long certain competencies are required and their potential return on investment – defining when to buy, build, or borrow. Plans better control operational costs, constantly mitigating the risks of hiring the wrong competencies in the wrong volumes for the wrong length of time. They also dynamically forecast real estate demand, enabling organisations to develop more cost-effective workplace strategies.

Appoint dedicated resource(s) to lead your strategic workforce plan, reshaping your talent supply and proactively closing critical skills gaps. Workforce planning leaders can model different workforce scenarios to help senior leaders make better data-driven decisions to control long-term costs. Invest in new technology that moves beyond generic business planning tools to enable faster, easier collaboration and rapid cycle planning. Ensure that workforce plans define and predict the cognitive abilities, social skills, and creative, problem-solving attributes that deliver competitive advantage.

Once businesses have defined all of the attributes critical to continued success, **measure the current competence of your workforce against them**. If that evaluation identifies a gap in supply, forecast the capability and speed of your employees to grow to fill that gap. This evaluation informs the updated approach to organisational learning, defining the training interventions needed to deliver ahead of demand (build) while identifying and prioritising the key gaps that TA teams must address over the long term (buy) and short term (borrow).

Finally, **extend planning to encompass the entire distributed workforce**. Track the competencies of your liquid workforce in real time to connect available supply to immediate demand, incentivising line managers to reduce barriers to horizontal movement. Identify additional valuable skills and experiences among existing independent workers and outsourced partners, aligning qualified capabilities to future projects. Require your external suppliers to have the essential values and behaviours that underpin your organisation's purpose, helping distributed teams to collaborate, innovate, and solve problems together.

Create demand across all supply

As talent aspirations change and human capital disengages from traditional talent attraction approaches, organisations have to find new ways to 'pull' top talent towards them. By investing in better talent experiences, relevant content, and a stronger, authentic online presence, organisations increase candidate and employee demand for their opportunities, improving the chances of finding and securing the best talent.

Start by **proactively rebuilding the experiences you want talent to have with your business**. Step inside your own talent journeys, understand workforce expectations, and reduce or remove barriers that undermine engagement.

> Use talent journey maps and talent analytics platforms such as Talentegy or Hotjar to identify the critical steps and assets that shape candidate, employee, and independent workers' talent experience.

For example, you could use simple mystery shopper campaigns to highlight critical bottlenecks or inconsistencies within the talent lifecycle, use design thinking in HR to clearly understand the target talent and engineer better experiences, and align fragmented HR software to strip out repetition and remove barriers to consistency.

Next, HR has to **create and share informative content that adds value to their target communities**. As discussed in *Chapter 7: Positioning for Success*, engaging content is not defined by what a company wants to say, but by what their target communities wants to know. Using social media surveys or leveraging internal and external networks to define demand, HR should create tailored content for each of their talent segments, configuring it for each context that their users consume it in, while curating its distribution to cut through the noise. This is particularly important to attract passive candidates, who often represent the highest quality and quantity of talent.

Finally, HR should focus much more on **proactively and authentically sharing the organisation's story.** As social media and independent third parties play a much more important role in shaping an organisation's reputation, HR must find new ways to indirectly influence all of their talent communities.

Encourage HR to shift from employment branding to talent branding, which *shows* – not tells – an organisation's story. By exploiting the shift in talent thinking and behaviour, talent branding leverages the authentic voice of active employees while empowering them to share more insights, more freely, and more publicly. This employee network connects with more indirect talent channels and authentically guides online influencers, pulling talent via peer-reviewed insights that provide social proof of emotional and ethical alignment.

HR can support this network with values-based stories using the right social media sharing buttons and well-crafted headlines. They should identify internal talent ambassadors who write honestly about their personal experience of the organisation's purpose and values. This means removing restrictions around social media use or incentivising distribution of stories through the employee referral program.

Proactively and constantly build communities and relationships

Just like consumer markets, talent markets are moving faster, served by many more channels, and bombarded with much more content. Talent pools are fragmenting, reforming around market challenges and opportunities instead of industries and geographies. To optimise talent supply, HR now has to connect to a wider range of platforms, proactively building communities and deeper relationships to create an ecosystem of followers, advocates, and pre-qualified candidates.

First, HR has to **connect to the new sharing platforms that serve your key talent segments**. Encourage TA to discover and join relevant online forums or networks. Incentivise core HR to build internal workforce networks that stretch horizontally across your business, identifying and engaging the critical talent that feeds your liquid workforce. Support HR, especially your TA function, to create new platforms to address untapped markets that may not already have an online community.

Next, HR should **build an authentic and benign presence within each key community**, nurturing the trust and credibility that indirectly drives engagement. TA should switch from 'mining' to 'farming' – cultivating talent communities by sharing useful content, such as non-sensitive market intelligence, or hosting topical Q&A sessions with company subject matter experts. Core HR can organise company-wide philanthropic initiatives aligned to the organisation's purpose or embed themselves in internal communities, removing barriers to collaboration, innovation, and horizontal movement. HR should position themselves as *enabling collaborators*, rather than recruitment salespeople or the policy police force.

Finally, HR needs to **invest in these communities**, developing a network of followers and an ecosystem of advocates that drives key talent towards them. Operating much like online community marketing managers, HR and TA teams should use social listening tools to monitor feedback and engagement, responding quickly and appropriately to requests. They should promote others in their networks, connecting community members where appropriate and helping employees or external talent to find information and answers quickly. As communities are in effect giant focus groups, HR can also use group conversations as feedback to continuously improve talent experiences and content across all their talent journeys.

Recommendation summary: Get ahead

To enable speed to value, HR has to get ahead of the demand curve – better understanding demand in order to shape supply. Just as marketing teams do for customers, HR needs to build deeper emotional connections with employees, independent workers and external talent to develop loyalty and underpin advocacy, connecting with more channels, constantly building trust and nurturing stronger relationships. They must continuously influence the company's employment reputation to maximise the chances of attracting the right talent at the right cost, positioning their organisation as a career partner that enables the long-term success of their workforces.

Recommendation 18: Liberate human capital to perform

Stronger, faster, connected infrastructure

HR systems need to shift away from a focus on transactional efficiency and move towards empowering businesses to make faster, better people decisions. Unfortunately, many HR infrastructures are subject to similar challenges outlined in the previous chapter, having been built to manage isolated transactional workflows and prioritise process efficiency. Data is often trapped in silos, with legacy HR management systems, ATSs, or Learning Management Systems (LMS) only able to provide limited historical reporting. Integrations with new high-value digital solutions are often hampered by technical or commercial restrictions of incumbent systems, which cannot always be replaced.

To leverage the full power of people data, **HR first needs to build a unified dataset**, integrating all of the people data from traditional HR silos and other business functions. Integration Platform as a Service (iPaaS) providers can potentially supply cost-effective solutions that work in conjunction with existing HR systems.

People strategy platforms such as Avature are designed to provide actionable strategic intelligence that leverages this data, better connecting people decisions to The Plan. For example, helping TA teams define and build the right talent communities long before they are needed. This unified data forms the bedrock for predictive analysis, rather than historical reporting.

Next, HR should **proactively streamline HR system interfaces with important or regular suppliers**. This means building connections to appropriate on-demand talent platforms while defining and embedding the right 'containers' in advance (see *Chapter 8: Operational Excellence*).

Companies like WorkMarket and Fieldglass offer contingent, gig, and project management tools so companies can effectively manage broader workforce ecosystems.[16] Xref uses blockchain technology to develop fast, mobile-friendly reference-checking products.[17]

Finally, HR systems should be configured to enable effective and productive collaboration across the entire distributed workforce. While many new communication tools such as Slack or Workplace by Facebook enable better connections across enterprises and networked project teams, these infrastructures need to *promote* rather than distract from productivity. HR must ensure that these communication tools **best support organisational objectives, defining principles and guidelines for their effective use** – and extending access to workforce segments outside your immediate business in order to improve communication and collaboration.

Augment HR with AI and automation

As operational demand, complexity, and volume increases, HR teams must leverage the revolution in technology and liberate themselves to focus on higher-value activities. Automation can pick up quantity task-focused workflows, freeing up HR teams to focus on strategic initiatives, while AI can improve speed and accuracy, helping HR teams to optimise their time.

HR can **leverage automation to deal with an increasing volume of people interactions**.

Spoke, a platform that manages workplace requests, uses an employee helpdesk smartbot to quickly provide knowledge and services to employees.[18] Zenefits' Slack integration allows workers to request time off via a chatbot without further manual entry.[19]

RPA can dramatically reduce both employees' and HR's time and efforts by completing data entry tasks across multiple HR systems, ensuring that essential data is captured and available.

AI can significantly augment TA efforts, crawling the web and scouring hundreds of sites including personal websites, meetup groups, and tech chat rooms to improve the speed and accuracy of talent searches. It can cross-analyse multiple data points against updated competency requirements to rapidly identify which talent is most likely to succeed.

Automated hiring and recruitment tools such as SmashFly use AI to reduce time to hire by accelerating the screening process.[20] Natural language processing (NLP) recruitment chatbots such as TextRecruit's Ari and Paradox.ai's Olivia ask intelligent questions and provide intelligent answers to avoid alienating candidates.[21]

Finally, HR should **invest in the technology that improves employee outcomes**.

Chatbots such as Spot, a harassment and discrimination reporting tool, can improve employee outcomes by removing bias and the fear of judgement that stops people from reporting incidents.[22]

Flexible workspace management software using 'activity-based working' allows distributed workforces to utilise office space optimally, simultaneously providing insights to better match demand to future real estate supply.

Always-on learning

HR must rethink its approach to career paths and L&D. Careers are no longer defined by slow-moving vertical succession plans but by fast-moving multi-directional development experiences. Effective long-term learning is essential to retain critical talent. Organisations should shift to an 'always-on' learning culture where workers can continually develop new skills and self-direct their education.

This change starts with L&D shifting its role away from administering transactional training to **empowering lifetime learning**. Encourage L&D teams to become flexible content curators, learning connectors, and cultural leaders, proactively building networks with new external suppliers to address high-demand competencies. L&D should act as learning catalysts, ensuring that they organise and share the best, most relevant content to targeted employees and teams. L&D's role is to inspire human capital to learn, develop the most valuable skills, and contribute to the learning of others.

Next, L&D needs to create an **always-on learning experience ecosystem** that connects human capital and learning supply with existing HR systems. Invest in an open platform that capitalises on the explosion in high-quality, low-cost, or free content available (such as Ted-Ed, MOOCs, or Udemy), while simultaneously allowing the workforce to share their learning across your organisation.

> As an example, GE created BrilliantYOU, "an online learning platform that features video-sharing and offers employee driven learning across the enterprise. In the first year, more than 30% of GE employees developed content and shared it with their peers."[23]

Also give non-permanent members of your workforce limited access to such platforms to encourage greater engagement and performance.

Finally, **empower individuals to constantly develop themselves**. Productivity improves when talented workers acquire new skills or sharpen existing ones. This in turn cultivates engagement and retention, creating a virtuous cycle of cost-effective performance returns. Enable more personalised learning solutions and liberate talent to move to different projects and teams, driving the cross-pollination of skills, experience, and thinking. A key role for HR in the digital age is to help employees identify their best next move.

> Grohappy provides personalised career support to employees, helping leaders to retain and motivate their talent.[24] IBM has created an AI-based self-assessment tool to help employees find training, job openings, and relevant career opportunities.[25]

Recommendation summary: Liberate human capital

Organisations need to invest in the technology that liberates HR to focus on creating commercial value, building a connected infrastructure that underpins their new role as business leaders, and streamlines collaboration and information-sharing. Businesses should augment existing HR practices and activities with AI and automation that enables HR to focus on the highest value activity while simultaneously improving employees' and candidates' talent experiences. Enterprises need to invest in lifetime learning, enabling their talent to continually grow and adapt to meet constantly changing demand.

Leveraging Human Capital

IMPACT OF FORCES		
I16. *Extract people value faster, dynamically, cost-effectively*	**I17.** *Changing value of human capital and HCM*	**I18.** *Changing HR operating realities*
Compressed timescales • Less time to galvanise teams to hit faster-moving targets • Less time to find, acquire, and deploy the right talent • Less time to upskill employees	**People increasing source of competitive advantage** • Customers buy from people they trust • Principal source of innovation • Across more points on the customer lifecycle	**Changing talent motivations** • Shift from passive resource to active asset • Organisational reputation critical • Human capital prioritises career development
Large permanent workforces carry more risk • Inflated balance sheet liabilities • Large real estate increasingly underutilised	**Changing skills demand and expanding skills gap** • New skills needed for different challenges • Demand for digital literacy growing • Traditional supply struggling to keep up	**Growing complexity** • Workforces more diverse, distributed, and discerning • Traditional attraction methods less effective • Workers expect personalised, immediate, and valuable experiences
Agile businesses depend on an agile workforce • Prescriptive people processes create drag • Multi-layer hierarchies increase steps • Internal metabolisms impact productive capacity	**Changing leader expectations** • Evolving definition of HR value • Commercial outcomes, not volume outputs	**Increased transactional demand** • Greater volume of people flowing in, through, and out of organisations • More internal talent movement across traditional boundaries • More responsive to more demands

RECOMMENDATIONS	ACTIVATE ➤	
R16. *Speed to value, not speed to service*	**R17.** *Get ahead of the curve*	**R18.** *Liberate human capital to perform*
Entrepreneurial HR • Think like investors • Identify areas of value creation and value at risk • Build commercial capability	**Build next-generation workforce planning** • Invest in continuously updated plan • Appoint a dedicated resource • Measure current competence of workforce • Apply to entire distributed workforce	**Stronger, faster, connected infrastructure** • Build unified dataset • Proactively streamline system interfaces with essential suppliers • Principles and guidelines for productive collaboration
Reposition HR • Senior leaders confront legacy barriers • Line managers reassume responsibility for people management • HR redefine new HR attributes	**Create demand across all supply** • Build the right talent experiences • Create and share valuable content • Proactively share your organisation's story	**Augment HR** • Automation to cope with growing volume of interactions • AI support talent acquisition • Technology to improve employee outcomes
Proactively reduce HR drag • Remove steps that don't deliver defined benefits • Apply processes proactively • Remove legacy barriers to engaging independent workers	**Proactively and constantly build talent communities** • Connect to key sharing platforms • Build a benign presence in key communities • Constantly invest in developing these communities	**Always-on learning** • Shift from transactional training to lifetime learning • Create an always-on learning ecosystem • Empower individuals to constantly develop themselves

ACTIVATE

Conclusion

1.

We have reached a tipping point.

To remain competitive, every company across every industry is being compelled to rethink its established ways of doing business. Change is set to continue and the ride is only going to get faster and the changes more fundamental. The risks of not adapting are starting to outweigh the risks of staying the same.

The tarnished state of the market economy means organisations can no longer focus exclusively on short-term rewards for shareholders, taking as much money as possible from society and putting as little back in. Now they are being forced to think beyond the quarterly balance sheet towards sustainable, long-term relevance.

Evolving stakeholder expectations, shifting economic landscapes, and disruptive new competitors means commercial success cannot be delivered through cost-cutting, production efficiency or fixed strategies. Instead, businesses must focus on customers rather than products, innovation rather than habit, trust rather than sales.

Technological advances, changing geopolitics and the evolving supply and demand of human capital mean profitability is no longer driven by even bigger, more vertically integrated businesses. Performance is no longer delivered though rigid processes, strict compliance and top-down command and control. Instead, organisations must now find ways to empower, rather than govern. To share rather than own. To collaborate, rather than compel.

Success in the digital age starts with embracing these new realities, understanding the various questions they raise, and developing different answers before it's too late.

The transformation timebomb is ticking.

2.

Nevertheless, among all the change and disruption, there is real opportunity. We have also learned that a few changes can make a world of difference. That organisations don't need to undo the past to be successful in the future, that they don't have to rip everything up and start again. That effective change can be simple, quick, and straightforward. That it doesn't have to be painful, potentially career-limiting, or high-risk.

Successful companies today are no more creative, intelligent or clairvoyant than the next. But by letting go of old habits, preconceptions, and fixed courses of action, many have found new ways to dramatically improve their performance, productivity, and profitability.

They have demonstrated that it is possible to create businesses that not only dynamically respond to their rapidly evolving environment but also improve performance and commitment through meaning and purpose. To engineer teams that autonomously make great decisions under pressure, while simultaneously building deeper, stronger customer relationships that drive loyalty, advocacy, and profitability. To empower their distributed workforce to collaborate effectively and get ahead of demand, improving productivity, and commercial relevance.

They are developing organisations that are able to change frequently and easily, are able to do many different things well, are versatile, flexible, multi-talented, and resourceful. They are creating 'The Protean Enterprise.'

3.

According to the Merriam-Webster online dictionary, *protean* is defined as:

1: of or resembling Proteus in having a varied nature or ability to assume different forms

2: displaying great diversity or variety. Versatile*

Over the course of the research and analysis throughout this book, some clear and consistent themes have emerged. While it remained obvious that no single solution could answer all the questions facing organisations, it became increasingly apparent that there are certain similarities in the way organisations can successfully *approach* the opportunities of the digital age. Several organisational attributes seem destined to play a much more important role in an organisation's ongoing success.

The Protean Enterprise is a hypothetical organisation that embodies these attributes. While it is unlikely that any business will be able to display all these qualities all of the time, the guidance below offers a useful blueprint to help model approaches, inform discussions, and guide decisions.

---

* 'protean' Merriam-Webster. https://www.merriam-webster.com/dictionary/protean

Showing, not telling: Protean enterprises are built on personal ownership and integrity. Leaders empower, rather than control. They don't tell teams what to do, they show them through their actions. They have the courage to say what needs to be said, both to the people they report to as well as the teams that report into them. They don't prioritise self-preservation, outsource essential initiatives to external consultants to reduce personal risk, or create a sense of plausible deniability if things go wrong.

Instead, they inspire performance through genuine, personal, long-term ownership and commitment. They are themselves transparent and expect transparency from those around them, cutting through internal politics to focus on what matters. They lead rather than manage, setting standards, role-modelling behaviours, and openly addressing the fear, misunderstandings, and misinterpretations that can derail their organisation's efforts.

Stop controlling, start inspiring: Protean enterprises have a clear purpose and an authentic identity. Leaders unify their entire distributed workforce with the clarity of their mission and the power of their purpose, supported by a culture that inspires self-sustaining performance. Protean businesses encourage questions, support curiosity, and share ownership, trusting and empowering each other to deliver The Plan.

Protean enterprises simplify and streamline their infrastructures and processes, removing unnecessary compliance and hierarchy to reduce drag, improve agility, and accelerate responsiveness. They liberate people to do their best work, while inspiring current and future decision-makers to constantly strive for better.

Prioritise sustainable relevance, not short-term returns: Protean enterprises commit to the long term, continuously planning for the future to get ahead of the demand curve. At the same time, they build in agility to quickly adapt to the here and now, remaining vigilant while preparing for impact. They concentrate on commercial relevance and sustainability, not because it looks good, but because it is fundamental to performance, productivity and profitability.

They focus on strategic results, not transactional tasks, deferring immediate gratification for long-term value creation. They measure outcomes, not just outputs, prioritising excellence over efficiency, and experience over service. They embrace sharing over owning, building dynamic supply that delivers higher quality at speed while paying only for what they need, when they need it. They invest in their future, spending money on the essential initiatives and assets that underpin long-term success.

Focus on trust and loyalty: Protean enterprises invest in positive long-term relationships with all their stakeholders – from customers and clients through to employees and external suppliers. They treat everyone as respected assets that grow in value, prioritising continuous and mutual long-term success to encourage loyalty, advocacy and commitment.

They build loyal communities and share their story openly and honestly, proactively shaping their reputation at the same time as fiercely guarding their customers' privacy. They collaborate rather than control and enable rather than exploit, leveraging their extended networks to capitalise on opportunities and defend against threats.

Always listening, always learning: Protean enterprises are open and dynamic. They connect to the right sources of information and embrace different perspectives, remaining open to new ideas, possibilities and opportunities. They embrace their changing reality, making time to listen to customers, colleagues and markets, understanding the causes as well as the symptoms of change.

They operate a virtuous cycle of listening and learning, using mistakes, failures and feedback as inspiration to adapt and improve. They invest time and resources to continually evolve, enabling their people to grow to meet the challenges of tomorrow as well as today.

4.

The road ahead is challenging. While individual transformation initiatives can be straightforward, the forces to stay the same are huge and hard to overcome. Creating an organisation that embraces change takes commitment, courage, tenacity, and no small amount of luck.

The first step is to raise awareness, which is what this book hopes to achieve. To share objective evidence and informed opinion to stimulate rational debate. While some may legitimately challenge the insights and recommendations contained in these pages, it is hoped closer examination of these critical issues will improve the collective commercial consciousness, fuelling improvements that benefit all those involved.

Try sharing this book or any of the other excellent titles out there (many of which have been referenced in this book). Forward relevant posts and articles onto your networks. Connect to appropriate external discussion groups and invite colleagues to join with you.

Next, start your own conversation. Focus on a few key individuals in your business and ask for their views. Target the cynics and antagonists as well as the cheerleaders and change champions. Create your own private community and invite your personal and professional contacts as well as trusted customers, partners, and suppliers.

Use the forum to test your intuition and accumulate your own objective evidence. Investigate the reactions to 'rocking the boat' and explore ways challenges can be overcome. Research which concepts and ideas resonate the loudest while inviting alternative suggestions.

Finally, make change an everyday activity in your business. Stop thinking of change as a separate intervention triggered in response to a specific event and start thinking of it as continuous adaptation to a constantly evolving environment. Move employees away from the perception of change as a negative force that they are forced to accept to a positive force that they can shape and own.

Make adaptation a key organisational behaviour, baking it into your company DNA. Update reward and incentive plans to encourage curiosity, vigilance, creativity, and experimentation. Don't delegate all change to external management consultants but instead make it part of everyone's role, particularly your senior leadership team.

5.

This book has not attempted to predict the future. Instead, it has tried to provide the tools, information, and insights to help leaders and decision-makers better prepare for the unknown. To ask questions, inspire ideas, and spark conversations. While we cannot know what the future holds, we can put ourselves in a better position to deal with it when it comes. By letting go of the past and believing that change is not only essential but positive, powerful, and above all profitable, leaders can build businesses capable of thriving for years to come.

Acknowledgements

Transformation Timebomb grew out of a series of conversations with a great number of people over several years. While it would it take too long to acknowledge all the kind people who have taken the time to share their wisdom, I would like to extend my sincerest appreciation to the following individuals in particular who have helped guide, inform, and illuminate the journey.

My thanks to Mick Axtell, Stephen Bates, Jean-Louis Bravard, Tom Chesterton, Andrew Cunningham, James Eve, Johnny Nicholls, Andrew Stewart, James Wight and Andy Wilkinson who not only agreed to give up their valuable time to be interviewed but who also shared some brilliant personal insights and fresh perspectives.

I'd also like to express my deep appreciation to Kenneth Gray, Carole Jackson, Nikki Marmery, Helen Rosethorn and Mark Wharrier for their support, ideas, and suggestions to help evolve and improve many of the concepts in the book. A considerable debt of gratitude must also be extended to Arthur and Jane Reay Jones who willingly lent their considerable talents to enlighten me in their field of expertise.

I would also like to thank Ross and Charlotte Dick-Cleland, Russell Fakira, Nick Jones, and Nina and Marcello Vendemiati for their wise counsel, honest feedback, and unquestioned support as I developed my thoughts and ideas. I cannot thank Elizabeth Weir enough for her guidance, encouragement, and candour in helping me make the finished book a reality.

Special thanks to my editor, Ameesha Smith-Green for her infinite patience, calmness, and undoubted expertise in distilling the finished manuscript.

Immeasurable appreciation must go to my amazing wife Claire, who above all others has shown incredible patience and unfailing support during my extended writing sabbatical, and to my three sons Fraser, Finlay, and Rory whose unbridled enthusiasm and boundless energy has been a constant source of inspiration. I couldn't have done any of this without all of you.

Finally, I owe my largest debt of gratitude to Neil Gray, without whom many of the ideas and concepts expressed in this book would never have come to fruition. Neil has given untold hours of his time, his prodigious intellect, and his unique perspective to help evolve the contents of these pages. Neil has forever changed the way I think about the business world, for which I will always be immensely grateful.

Author biography

Gavin Russell is the co-founder of Agora Cubed, a business evolution consultancy, along with Neil Gray. He has 20 years' experience in change management, predominantly in the talent acquisition industry. He has lived and worked in the UK, France, and Australia and advised both B2B and B2C organisations ranging from 100 to 250,000 employees. He lives in Buckinghamshire, UK and blogs at **www.gavinrussellconnect.com**.

Notes

Chapter 1

[1] Elliot, Larry; Partington, Richard; Helmore, Edward. "US on brink of trade war with EU, Canada and Mexico as tit-for-tat tariffs begin." *The Guardian* Newspaper. 31 May 2018. https://www.theguardian.com/business/2018/may/31/us-fires-opening-salvo-in-trade-war-with-eu-canada-and-mexico

[2] Subramaniam, Vanmala. "Bombardier's C Series jets slapped with 220% tax, making them virtually unsellable." *Vice Money*. 27 September 2017. https://news.vice.com/en_ca/article/wjz4qy/bombardiers-c-series-jets-slapped-with-220-tax-making-them-virtually-unsellable

[3] Jones, Marc. "World has racked up 7,000 protectionist measures since crisis: study." *Reuters Business News*. 15 November 2017 https://uk.reuters.com/article/us-global-economy-protectionism/world-has-racked-up-7000-protectionist-measures-since-crisis-study-idUKKBN1DF005

[4] Liesman, Steve. "Trump economic 'uncertainty' worse than '08 financial crisis levels, index shows." *CNBC*. 19 May 2017. https://www.cnbc.com/2017/05/18/economic-uncertainty-index-surpasses-08-financial-crisis-levels.html

[5] "Two years and counting: Optimism dives again in Financial Services – CBI/PwC." *CBI*. 26 March 2018. https://www.cbi.org.uk/media-centre/articles/two-years-and-counting-optimism-dives-again-in-financial-services-cbipwc/

[6] Kose. Ayhan. "Global Economy in 2017: Hope and Uncertainty." *The World Bank*. 15 February 2017. http://www.worldbank.org/en/news/opinion/2017/02/15/global-economy-in-2017-hope-and-uncertainty

[7] "Importance of Fossil Fuels." *International Association of Geophysical Contractors* (IAGC). https://www.iagc.org/importance-of-fossil-fuels.html

[8] Rifkin, Jeremy. "The Third Industrial Revolution: A Radical New Sharing Economy." *Vice*. 13 February 2018. https://www.youtube.com/watch?v=QX3M8Ka9vUA

[9] "When will fossil fuel run out?" *NRGExpert Energy Intelligence*. 24 September 2012. https://www.nrgexpert.com/when-will-fossil-fuel-run-out/

[10] Slav, Irina. "OPEC Threatens to Kill U.S. Shale." *Oilprice.com*. 14 March 2019 https://oilprice.com/Geopolitics/International/OPEC-Threatens-To-Kill-US-Shale.html

[11] Davies, Rob; and agencies. "Air pollution fears see demand for diesel cars fall by fifth." *The Guardian* Newspaper. 5 June 2017. https://www.theguardian.com/environment/2017/jun/05/air-pollution-fears-demand-diesel-cars-fall-fifth

[12] McGrath, Matt. "Final call to save the world from 'climate catastrophe'." *BBC News*. 8 October 2018 https://www.bbc.co.uk/news/science-environment-45775309

[13] *Wikipedia*. "Paris Agreement" https://en.wikipedia.org/wiki/Paris_Agreement

[14] Harrabin, Roger. "Climate change: 'Right to repair' gathers force." *BBC News*. 9 January 2019. https://www.bbc.co.uk/news/science-environment-46797396

[15] McKinsey Global Institute. "Solving the Productivity Puzzle: The role of demand and the promise of digitization." *McKinsey & Company*. February 2018. https://www.mckinsey.com/~/media/mckinsey/featured%20insights/meeting%20societys%20expectations/solving%20the%20productivity%20puzzle/mg-solving-the-productivity-puzzle--report-february-2018.ashx

16 Rifkin, Jeremy. "The Third Industrial Revolution: A Radical New Sharing Economy." *Vice*. 13 February 2018. https://www.youtube.com/watch?v=QX3M8Ka9vUA

17 "2017 Edelman Trust Barometer." *Edelman*. 21 January 2017. https://www.edelman.com/research/2017-edelman-trust-barometer

18 Afshar, Vala. "New Research Uncovers Big Shifts in Customer Expectations and Trust." *Salesforce Research*. 5 June 2018. https://www.salesforce.com/blog/2018/06/digital-customers-research.html

19 Shane, Scott; Wakabayashi, Daisuke. "'The Business of War': Google Employees Protest Work for the Pentagon." *The New York Times*. 4 April 2018. https://www.nytimes.com/2018/04/04/technology/google-letter-ceo-pentagon-project.html

20 Barford, Vanessa; Holt, Gerry. "Google, Amazon, Starbucks: The rise of 'tax shaming'." *BBC News* Magazine 21 May 2013. https://www.bbc.co.uk/news/magazine-20560359

21 Fink, Larry. "A Sense of Purpose." *Blackrock*. January 2018. https://www.blackrock.com/corporate/investor-relations/2018-larry-fink-ceo-letter

Chapter 2

1 Birkner, Christine. "How Delta's Focus on Customer Experience Turned a Bankrupt Airline into a Powerhouse Brand." *Adweek*. 9 April 2017 https://www.adweek.com/brand-marketing/how-deltas-focus-on-customer-experience-created-a-powerhouse-brand/

2 Whitler, Kimberly A. "From Product-Centricity to Consumer-Centricity: A Shift At One Of The World's Largest Tech Companies." *Forbes*. 9 Jan 2016. https://www.forbes.com/sites/kimberlywhitler/2016/01/09/from-product-centricity-to-consumer-centricity-a-shift-at-one-of-the-worlds-largest-tech-companies/#5b68da15ebf8

3 LeBeau, Phil. "Car-sharing a growing threat to auto sales: Study." *CNBC*. 4 Feb 2014. https://www.cnbc.com/2014/02/04/car-sharing-a-growing-threat-to-auto-sales-study.html

4 "By 2030, the transport sector will require 138 million fewer cars in Europe and the US." *PwC Press Room*. 16 January 2018. https://press.pwc.com/News-releases/by-2030--the-transport-sector-will-require-138-million-fewer-cars-in-europe-and-the-us/s/a624f0b2-453d-45a0-9615-f4995aaaa6cb

5 Cannon, Damian. "Fever-Tree: Creating an Iconic brand." *Stockopedia*. 3 May 2017. https://www.stockopedia.com/content/fever-tree-creating-an-iconic-brand-182256/

6 *The Week Magazine*. July 2018

7 "The world's most valuable resource is no longer oil, but data." *The Economist*. 6 May 2017. https://www.economist.com/leaders/2017/05/06/the-worlds-most-valuable-resource-is-no-longer-oil-but-data

8 Patrizio, Andy. "IDC: Expect 175 zettabytes of data worldwide by 2025." *Network World*. 3 December 2018. https://www.networkworld.com/article/3325397/idc-expect-175-zettabytes-of-data-worldwide-by-2025.html

9 Huff, Stanley M.D. "Open data sharing will improve care, lower costs." *AthenaInsight*. 16 February 2017. https://www.athenahealth.com/insight/open-data-sharing-will-improve-care-lower-costs

10 u/Balance "Tesla is uploading huge amounts of autopilot data from their cars to their servers, which helps train AP. But maybe they should give their superchargers a fast internet connection for those with slow upload or data caps." *Reddit*. 2018. https://www.reddit.com/r/teslamotors/comments/7bhia4/tesla_is_uploading_huge_amounts_of_autopilot_data/

11 West, Darrell M.; Allen, John R. "How artificial intelligence is transforming the world." *Brookings*. 24 April 2018. https://www.brookings.edu/research/how-artificial-intelligence-is-transforming-the-world/

[12] Hsu, Tiffany. "For Many Facebook Users, a 'Last Straw' That Led Them to Quit." *The New York Times*. 21 March 2018. https://www.nytimes.com/2018/03/21/technology/users-abandon-facebook.html

[13] Chui, Michael; Manyika, James; Miremadi, Mehdi. "Where machines could replace humans-and where they can't (yet)." *McKinsey Digital*. July 2016. https://www.mckinsey.com/business-functions/digital-mckinsey/our-insights/where-machines-could-replace-humans-and-where-they-cant-yet

[14] "Liquid Workforce: Building the workforce for today's digital demands." *Accenture Technology Vision 2016*. https://www.accenture.com/fr-fr/_acnmedia/PDF-2/Accenture-Liquid-Workforce-Technology-Vision-2016-france.pdf

[15] 'WeWork.' *Wikipedia*. https://en.wikipedia.org/wiki/WeWork

[16] Power, Brad. "How GE Applies Lean Startup Practices." *Harvard Business Review*. 23 April 2014. https://hbr.org/2014/04/how-ge-applies-lean-startup-practices

[17] Kendis team. "Exploring Key Elements of Spotify's Agile Scaling Model." *Medium.com*. 23 July 2018. https://medium.com/@media_75624/exploring-key-elements-of-spotifys-agile-scaling-model-471d2a23d7ea

Chapter 3

[1] Ettinger, Jill. "McDonald's UK launches Vegan Happy Meals." *Livekindly*. 3 January 2019. https://www.livekindly.co/mcdonalds-uk-vegan-happy-meals-dairy-free-pesto/

[2] "Global Workforce by 2020, by generation." *Statista*. December 2016. https://www.statista.com/statistics/829705/global-employment-by-generation/

[3] Hall, Mark. "What The Ideal Workplace Of The Future Looks Like, According to Millennials." *Forbes*. 8 November 2017. https://www.forbes.com/sites/markhall/2017/11/08/what-the-ideal-workplace-of-the-future-looks-like-according-to-millennials/#135624294228

[4] Miller, Lee J; Lu, Wei. "Gen Z Is Set to Outnumber Millennials Within a Year." *Bloomberg*. 20 August 2018. https://www.bloomberg.com/news/articles/2018-08-20/gen-z-to-outnumber-millennials-within-a-year-demographic-trends

[5] "How Millennials Want to Work and Live." *Gallup Workplace*. 2016. https://www.gallup.com/workplace/238073/millennials-work-live.aspx

[6] "The Deloitte Millennial Survey 2018." *Deloitte*. 2018. https://www2.deloitte.com/global/en/pages/about-deloitte/articles/millennialsurvey.html

[7] Alton, Larry. "Are Remote Workers More Productive Than In-Office Workers?" *Forbes*. 7 March 2017. https://www.forbes.com/sites/larryalton/2017/03/07/are-remote-workers-more-productive-than-in-office-workers/#73926eb131f6

[8] "Developing legal talent. Stepping into the future law firm." *Deloitte*. February 2016. https://www2.deloitte.com/uk/en/pages/audit/articles/developing-legal-talent.html

[9] Frey, Carl Benedikt; Osborne, Michael A. "The Future of Employment: How susceptible are jobs to computerisation." *Oxford Martin School, University of Oxford*. 17 September 2013 https://www.oxfordmartin.ox.ac.uk/downloads/academic/The_Future_of_Employment.pdf

[10] Arlidge, John. "What will happen when robots take our jobs?" *The Sunday Times Magazine*. 27 August 2017. https://www.thetimes.co.uk/article/what-will-happen-when-robots-take-our-jobs-ai-pglfwmxmw

[11] McKinsey Global Institute. "Independent Work: Choice, Necessity and the Gig Economy." *McKinsey & Company*. October 2016. https://www.mckinsey.com/~/media/McKinsey/Featured%20Insights/Employment%20and%20Growth/Independent%20work%20Choice%20necessity%20and%20the%20gig%20economy/Independent-Work-Choice-necessity-and-the-gig-economy-Full-report.ashx

[12] "Freelancing in America 2017." *Edelman Intelligence* 2017. https://www.upwork.com/i/freelancing-in-america/2017/

[13] Warr, Peter; Inceoglu, Iike. "Work Orientations, Well-Being and Job Content of Self-Employed and Employed Professionals." *Sage Journals*. 21 August 2017. https://journals.sagepub.com/doi/abs/10.1177/0950017017717684?journalCode=wesa

[14] 'Definitive Study of The Self-Employed' Reveals They Make £33K Average Annual Revenues, Work Less and are Happier Than Salaried Workers." *Global Banking and Finance Review*. 27 January 2017. https://www.globalbankingandfinance.com/definitive-study-of-the-self-employed-reveals-they-make-33k-average-annual-revenues-work-less-and-are-happier-than-salaried-workers/

[15] "2017 MBO Partners State of Independence in America: Today's Independents Are Happier, Healthier, and More Satisfied Than Ever Before." *MBO Partners Independent Workforce Trends*. 13 June 2017. https://www.mbopartners.com/blog/independent-workforce-trends/2017-mbo-partners-state-of-independence-in-america-todays-independents-are-happier-healthier-and-more-satisfied-than-ever-before/

[16] McKinsey Global Institute. "Independent Work: Choice, Necessity and the Gig Economy." *McKinsey & Company*. October 2016. https://www.mckinsey.com/~/media/McKinsey/Featured%20Insights/Employment%20and%20Growth/Independent%20work%20Choice%20necessity%20and%20the%20gig%20economy/Independent-Work-Choice-necessity-and-the-gig-economy-Full-report.ashx

[17] Pofeldt, Elaine. "New Study: Why Self-Employment Keeps Accelerating." *Forbes*. 13 June 2017. https://www.forbes.com/sites/elainepofeldt/2017/06/13/new-study-why-self-employment-keeps-accelerating/#54c6ad7d6ac8

[18] Taylor, Matthew. "Good work: the Taylor review if modern working practices." *UK Government*. 11 July 2017. https://www.gov.uk/government/publications/good-work-the-taylor-review-of-modern-working-practices

[19] "The Harmonization Project." *Coalition to Promote Independent Entrepreneurs*. 2019. https://iccoalition.org/the-harmonization-project/

Chapter 4

[1] "New car models have a shorter 'shelf-life' than ever, says CAP." *Automotive Management Online – Supplier News*. 23 May 2013. https://www.am-online.com/news/2013/5/23/new-car-models-have-a-shorter-shelf-life-than-ever-says-cap/32983/

[2] Nichols, JP. "Your Fast Follower Strategy is Riskier Than You Realise." *JPNichols.com*. 8 February 2016. http://jpnicols.com/2016/02/08/fast_follower/

[3] Milliken, David; Taylor, Edward. "BMW executive says would shut UK plants if Brexit hits supply chain." *Reuters*. 25 June 2018. https://uk.reuters.com/article/us-britain-eu-bmw/bmw-executive-says-would-shut-uk-plants-if-brexit-hits-supply-chain-idUKKBN1JL23K

[4] "Jaguar Land Rover posts £34.4bn loss as China demand slips." *BBC Business*. 7 February 2019. https://www.bbc.co.uk/news/business-47155145

[5] Nicolaci da Costa, Ana. "The early victims of Trump's trade war." *BBC Business*. 5 August 2018. https://www.bbc.co.uk/news/business-45028014

[6] Appleby, Kyra. "Five cities proving that we can quit fossil fuels." *CityMetric*. 6 October 2015. https://www.citymetric.com/horizons/five-cities-proving-we-can-quit-fossil-fuels-1444

[7] Dienel, Eva. "The 3 business risks of using fossil fuels." *GreenBiz*. 6 April 201. https://www.greenbiz.com/article/3-business-risks-using-fossil-fuels

[8] "We Analyzed 12 Of The Biggest Direct-to-Consumer Success Stories to Figure Out The Secrets To Their Growth – Here's What We Learned." *CBInsights Research Brief*. 6 February 2019. https://www.cbinsights.com/research/direct-to-consumer-retail-strategies/

[9] Cassar, Ken. "Brands selling direct" What does Unilever's $1 billion bet tell us?" *Digital Commerce 360*. 21 July 2016. https://www.digitalcommerce360.com/2016/07/21/brands-selling-direct-what-does-unilevers-1-billion-bet-say/

[10] Kalms, Brian. "Retailers should fear a more direct approach." *ElixIRR*. 1 May 2018. https://www.elixirr.com/2018/05/with-more-consumer-packaged-goods-companies-going-direct-to-consumer/

[11] Read, Simon. "Millions overcharged for mobile contracts." *BBC Business*. 19 September 2018. https://www.bbc.co.uk/news/business-45561044

[12] Reuters. "State Street fined $38 million for overcharging clients." *CNBC*. 31 January 2014. https://www.cnbc.com/2014/01/31/state-street-fined-38-million-for-overcharging-clients.html

[13] Morgan, Lisa. "Big Data: 6 Real-Life Business Cases." *Information Week*. 27 May 2015. https://www.informationweek.com/software/enterprise-applications/big-data-6-real-life-business-cases/d/d-id/1320590?image_number=2

[14] Goldman, David. "Nike's Colin Kaepernick gamble is already paying off." *CNN Business*. 14 September 2018. https://money.cnn.com/2018/09/14/news/companies/nike-kaepernick/index.html

[15] Feloni, Richard; Ciolli, Joe. "Iconic hedge fund billionaire Seth Klarman explains why traditional business models are broken and outlines how companies can fix them." *Business Insider*. 28 November 2018. https://www.businessinsider.com/business-models-are-broken-how-to-fix-them-seth-klarman-2018-11?r=UK

[16] Baird, Ross. "Why this institutional investor's impact play matters." *Medium*. 13 November 2017. https://medium.com/village-capital/why-this-institutional-investors-impact-play-is-a-big-deal-6603892dce90

[17] Brown, Cristan. "How to become truly customer-centric: 4 examples from the tech industry." *Vision Critical*. 27 April 2019. https://www.visioncritical.com/blog/how-to-become-truly-customer-centric-4-examples-from-the-tech-industry

[18] Crook, Jordan. "Lemonade wants to rewrite the insurance policy itself." *TechCrunch*. 2018. https://techcrunch.com/2018/05/16/lemonade-wants-to-rewrite-the-insurance-policy-itself/?guccounter=1

[19] Morgan, Blake. "5 Fresh Examples of Customer Experience Innovation." *Forbes*. 17 July 2017. https://www.forbes.com/sites/blakemorgan/2017/07/17/5-fresh-examples-of-customer-experience-innovation/#688d5ab45c18

[20] Stone, Madeline. "Amazon has rolled out its 'try before you buy' shopping service to all Prime members. Here's what it's like to use." *Business Insider*. 6 July 2018. https://www.businessinsider.com/amazon-prime-wardrobe-how-to-use-2018-7?r=UK

[21] "Zara supply chain analysis – the secret behind Zara's retail success." *Tradegecko*. 25 June 2018. https://www.tradegecko.com/blog/zara-supply-chain-its-secret-to-retail-success

[22] Anthony, Scott. "3 Ways To Predict What Consumers Want Before The Know It." *Fast Company*. 16 February 2012. https://www.fastcompany.com/1669070/3-ways-to-predict-what-consumers-want-before-they-know-it

[23] Jiao, Gene. "Why The Consumer is Huawei's Catalyst For Constant Innovation And Development." *Entrepreneur*. 12 April 2018. https://www.entrepreneur.com/article/311807

[24] Davies, Rob. "Jaguar Land Rover to shut Solihull plant for two weeks after China sales slump." *The Guardian*. 8 October 2018. https://www.theguardian.com/business/2018/oct/08/jaguar-land-rover-to-shut-solihull-plant-for-two-weeks-after-china-sales-slump

[25] Franck, Thomas. "Tesla shares slip after report says China sales sank 70% in October." *CNBC Markets*. 27 November 2018. https://www.cnbc.com/2018/11/27/tesla-shares-drop-2percent-after-report-says-china-sales-sank-70percent-in-october.html

[26] "Connecting the dots: how purpose can join up your business." *PwC*. https://www.pwc.com/gx/en/ceo-agenda/pulse/purpose.html#Purpose

[27] Niket. 'The Fundamentals. Objectives and Key Results." *Medium*. 28 November 2014. https://medium.com/startup-tools/okrs-5afdc298bc28

[28] Barton, Dominic; Wiseman, Mark. "Focusing Capital on the Long Term." *Harvard Business Review*. January-February 2014. https://hbr.org/2014/01/focusing-capital-on-the-long-term

[29] Barton, Dominic. "Capitalism for the long term." *Harvard Business Review*. March 2011. https://hbr.org/2011/03/capitalism-for-the-long-term

[30] Barton, Dominic; Wiseman, Mark. "Focusing Capital on the Long Term." Harvard Business Review. January-February 2014. https://hbr.org/2014/01/focusing-capital-on-the-long-term

Chapter 5

[1] Frei, Frances; Morriss, Anne. "Culture Takes Over When the CEO Leaves the Room." *Harvard Business Review*. 10 May 2012. https://hbr.org/2012/05/culture-takes-over-when-the-ce

[2] "Organizational Culture." Business Dictionary. *WebFinance Inc*. http://www.businessdictionary.com/definition/organizational-culture.html

[3] Oswald, Andrew J; Proto, Eugenio; Sgroi, Daniel. "New study shows we work harder when we are happy." *University of Warwick, Department of Economics*. 21 March 2014. https://warwick.ac.uk/newsandevents/pressreleases/new_study_shows/

[4] "What Your Disaffected Workers Cost." *Gallup Business Journal*. 15 March 2001. https://news.gallup.com/businessjournal/439/what-your-disaffected-workers-cost.aspx

[5] Schwartz, Tony. "The Productivity Paradox: How Sony Pictures Gets More Out of People by Demanding Less." *Harvard Business Review*. June 2010. https://hbr.org/2010/06/the-productivity-paradox-how-sony-pictures-gets-more-out-of-people-by-demanding-less

[6] Kalish, Alyse. "It's True: Happy People Are Just More Productive." *The Muse*. https://www.themuse.com/advice/its-true-happy-people-are-just-more-productive

[7] Dymock, Alan. "Why are the All Blacks so good." *CNN*. 19 July 2018. https://edition.cnn.com/2018/07/18/sport/new-zealand-rugby-all-blacks-rugby-world-cup/index.html

[8] Sinek, Simon. "How great leaders inspire action." *TEDx Puget Sound*. September 2009. https://www.ted.com/talks/simon_sinek_how_great_leaders_inspire_action/up-next?language=en

[9] Hyken, Shep. "How Happy Employees Make Happy Customers." *Forbes*. 27 May 2017. https://www.forbes.com/sites/shephyken/2017/05/27/how-happy-employees-make-happy-customers/#130700715c35

[10] Madupu, Sareen Babu. "6 easy ways for Creating a culture of Innovation in the workplace." *Acuvate*. 16 May 2018. https://acuvate.com/blog/creating-driving-culture-innovation-workplace/

[11] Williams, David K. "Brad Smith, Intuit CEO: How To Be A Great Leader: Get Out Of The Way." *Forbes*. 25 June 2012. https://www.forbes.com/sites/davidkwilliams/2012/06/25/growing-a-company-qa-with-brad-smith-intuit-ceo-remove-the-barriers-to-innovation-and-get-out-of-the-way/#12aba81b1ff5

[12] Goran, Julie; LaBerge, Laura; Srinivasan, Ramesh. "Culture for a digital age." *McKinsey Quarterly*. July 2017. https://www.mckinsey.com/business-functions/digital-mckinsey/our-insights/culture-for-a-digital-age

[13] Caramela, Sammi. "Money Isn't Enough: 4 Incentives to Motivate Your Employees." *Business News Daily*. 7 May 2018. https://www.businessnewsdaily.com/10731-money-not-enough.html

[14] Misa, Nick. "The Top 5 Sites for Employer Reviews & Ratings." *Ongig*. 25 June 2016. https://blog.ongig.com/employer-branding/the-top-5-sites-for-employer-reviews-ratings

[15] Lawler, Ryan. "Memo Brings Anonymous Group Sharing To The Enterprise." *TechCrunch*. 2015. https://techcrunch.com/2015/01/16/memo/?guccounter=1

[16] Hull, Kristy. "Getting to the Critical Few Behaviours That Can Drive Cultural Change." *Strategy+business*. 22 May 2017. https://www.strategy-business.com/blog/Getting-to-the-Critical-Few-Behaviors-That-Can-Drive-Cultural-Change?gko=463e5

[17] Mueller, Rene. Dr. "How to Communicate Your Company's Core Values and Work Culture." *Qnnect*. 6 April 2017. https://www.qnnect.com/blog/how-to-communicate-your-companys-core-values-and-work-culture

[18] Humphrey, Chris; Macdonald, Emma. "Why a people-centred culture is crucial in the digital age." *Ethical Corporation*. 30 July 2018. http://www.ethicalcorp.com/why-people-centred-culture-crucial-digital-age

Chapter 6

[1] "Organizational Structure." *The Business Dictionary*. http://www.businessdictionary.com/definition/organizational-structure.html

[2] "Organizational Leadership." *The Business Dictionary*. http://www.businessdictionary.com/definition/organizational-leadership.html

[3] Corkindale, Gill. "The Importance of Organizational Design and Structure." *Harvard Business Review*. 11 February 2011. https://hbr.org/2011/02/the-importance-of-organization

[4] Bloch, Nicolas; Hadley, James; Lancry, Ouriel; Lundqvist, Jenny. "Strategy Beyond Scale." *Bain & Company*. 11 February 2015. https://www.bain.com/insights/strategy-beyond-scale

[5] Fernando, Vincent. "Blame Toyota's Disaster On Japanese Corporate Culture." *Business Insider*. 6 February 2010. https://www.businessinsider.com/blame-toyotas-disaster-on-japanese-corporate-culture-2010-2?r=US&IR=T

[6] Ro, Sam. "Aluminum giant Alcoa is splitting itself in 2." Business Insider. 28 September 2015. https://www.businessinsider.com/alcoa-to-separate-into-two-companies-2015-9?r=US&IR=T

[7] "Chapter 7. Organisational Structure and Change." Saylor.org Academy. https://resources.saylor.org/wwwresources/archived/site/wp-content/uploads/2011/06/BUS208-5.4.pdf

[8] Morgan, Blake. "The 10 Most Customer-Obsessed Companies in 2018." *Forbes*. 15 February 2018. https://www.forbes.com/sites/blakemorgan/2018/02/15/the-10-most-customer-obsessed-companies-in-2018/#6d2a02286ba1

[9] Denning, Steve. "Why Agile Is Eating The World." *Forbes*. 2 January 2018. https://www.forbes.com/sites/stevedenning/2018/01/02/why-agile-is-eating-the-world%E2%80%8B%E2%80%8B/#293b95e54a5b

[10] Sutton, Danielle. "Human-Centred Design: How to Embrace Failing Fast." *+Acumen*. 20 June 2018. https://www.plusacumen.org/journal/human-centered-design-how-embrace-failing-fast

[11] "Dunbar's number." *Wikipedia*. https://en.wikipedia.org/wiki/Dunbar%27s_number

[12] 'What is Holacracy.' *Holacracy.org*. https://www.holacracy.org/what-is-holacracy

[13] Murphy, Mark. "The Leadership Model Used By Steve Jobs, Henry Ford and Thomas Edison." *Forbes*. 14 January 2018. https://www.forbes.com/sites/markmurphy/2018/01/14/the-leadership-model-used-by-steve-jobs-henry-ford-and-thomas-edison/#2b88d87923f6

Chapter 7

[1] "Promotion (marketing)". *Wikipedia*. https://en.wikipedia.org/wiki/Promotion_(marketing)

[2] 'Unilever Consumer Study Shows A Third Of Consumers Prefer Brands Doing Social or Environmental Good." *Engage for Good*. 5 January 2017. https://engageforgood.com/unilever-consumer-study-shows-third-consumers-prefer-brands-social-environmental-good/

[3] Litsa, Tereza. "Brand activism: Why more campaigns focus on social good." *ClickZ*. 9 February 2018. https://www.clickz.com/brand-activism-campaigns-focus-social-good/207888/

[4] "Innovation of the Day: Volvo." *Trend Watching*. 4 March 2019. http://info.trendwatching.com/fishing-for-trash-for-the-fish?utm_campaign=Innovation%20of%20the%20Day%20&utm_source=hs_email&utm_medium=email&utm_content=70415496&_hsenc=p2ANqtz--LiszTDjlxLJ9RjHcTJL4yzLv9PFPKSUqmVA_N_YVQHixJvGpuiL3mlYJNwr2VNGGw19tZnhedmfYxmwCkf7R1-4icZQ

[5] "10 Zappos Stories That Will Change the Way You Look at Customer Service Forever." *Infinit-O*. 28 October 2013. https://resourcecenter.infinit-o.com/blog/zappos-stories-that-will-change-the-way-you-look-at-customer-service

[6] Ziliani, Cristina. "Smart consumers, smart loyalty: How the digital revolution transforms customer retention." *Sabre*. 15 June 2017. https://www.sabre.com/insights/smart-consumers-smart-loyalty-how-the-digital-revolution-transforms-customer-retention/

[7] Harvey, Steve. "Let's be honest: Brand transparency and consumer trust." *Fabrik Brands*. 20 April 2018. http://fabrikbrands.com/brand-transparency-and-consumer-trust/

[8] Kline, Kenny. "Here's How Important Brand Transparency Is for Your Business." *Inc*. 7 September 2016. https://www.inc.com/kenny-kline/new-study-reveals-just-how-important-brand-transparency-really-is.html

[9] Kilgore, Tomi; Linnane, Ciara; Johnson, Angela; Booton, Jennifer. "7 companies hurt by bad publicity." *MarketWatch*. 18 August 2014. https://www.marketwatch.com/story/7-companies-hurt-by-bad-publicity-2014-08-18

[10] "Weinstein Company files for bankruptcy." *BBC News*. 20 March 2018. https://www.bbc.co.uk/news/world-us-canada-43466469

[11] Elgot, Jessica; McVeigh, Karen. "Oxfam loses 7,000 donors since sexual exploitation scandal." *The Guardian*. 20 February 2018. https://www.theguardian.com/world/2018/feb/20/oxfam-boss-mark-goldring-apologises-over-abuse-of-haiti-quake-victims

[12] "The Ranking Digital Rights 2018 Corporate Accountability Index." *Ranking Digital Rights*. April 2018. https://rankingdigitalrights.org/index2018/

[13] Bisson, David. "Why Consumers Demand Greater Transparency Around Data Privacy." *Security Intelligence*. 17 July 2018. https://securityintelligence.com/news/why-consumers-demand-greater-transparency-around-data-privacy/

[14] Allen, Robert. "What happens online in 60 seconds." *Smart Insights*. 6 February 2017. https://www.smartinsights.com/internet-marketing-statistics/happens-online-60-seconds/

[15] Schaefer, Mark. "Content Shock: Why content marketing is not a sustainable strategy." *Mark Schaefer.* https://businessesgrow.com/2014/01/06/content-shock/

[16] "Banner blindness." *Wikipedia.* https://en.wikipedia.org/wiki/Banner_blindness

[17] Martin. "Spotify Online Music Platform." *Cleverism.* 3 November 2014. https://www.cleverism.com/spotify-online-music-platform/

[18] Brody, Deborah. "Why Uber is successful." *Deborah Brody Marketing Communications.* https://deborahbrody.com/2013/07/why-uber-is-successful/

[19] Lewis, Bill. "The Digital Mesh – You Must Understand it To Survive It." *BBN Times.* 30 January 2018. https://www.bbntimes.com/en/companies/the-digital-mesh-you-must-understand-it-to-survive

[20] Del Gigante, Michael. "How Social Media Has Changed The Ad Game." *MDG Advertising.* 12 July 2018. https://www.mdgadvertising.com/marketing-insights/infographics/how-social-media-changed-the-ad-game-infographic/

[21] McCue, TJ. "Social Media is Increasing Brand Engagement And Sales." *Forbes.* 26 June 2018. https://www.forbes.com/sites/tjmccue/2018/06/26/social-media-is-increasing-brand-engagement-and-sales/#5f3c19ce7cb3

[22] "7 Great B2B Influencer Marketing Examples." *Influencer Marketing Hub.* https://influencermarketinghub.com/7-great-b2b-influencer-marketing-examples/

[23] Birkett, Alex. "How User Generated Reviews Affect Conversion Rates." *ConversionXL.* 25 May 2016. https://conversionxl.com/blog/user-generated-reviews/

[24] Causon, Jo. "Customer complaints made via social media on the rise." *The Guardian.* 21 May 2015. https://www.theguardian.com/media-network/2015/may/21/customer-complaints-social-media-rise

[25] Young, Heike. "New Data: The Connected Customer's Wants and Needs in 2017." *Salesforce.* 4 January 2017. https://www.salesforce.com/blog/2017/01/data-the-connected-customers-wants.html

[26] Bonchek, Mark; Bapat, Vivek. "The Most Successful Brands Focus on Users – Not Buyers." *Harvard Business Review.* 7 February 2018. https://hbr.org/2018/02/the-most-successful-brands-focus-on-users-not-buyers

[27] Longanecker, Chuck. "Customer Experience Is the Future of Design." *UX Magazine.* 19 February 2016. https://uxmag.com/articles/customer-experience-is-the-future-of-design

[28] Ripsam, Thomas; Bouquet, Louis. "10 Principals of Customer Strategy." *Strategy+business.* 26 September 2016. https://www.strategy-business.com/article/10-Principles-of-Customer-Strategy?gko=083a5

[29] McClafferty, Alex. "Customer Success: The Best Kept Secret of Hyper-Growth Startups." *Forbes.* 18 May 2015. https://www.forbes.com/sites/alexmcclafferty/2015/05/18/customer-success/#266c1171777a

[30] Richman, Jonha. "5 examples of Companies Succeeding Through Transparency." *Entrepreneur Europe.* 27 May 2016. https://www.entrepreneur.com/article/274636

[31] "Kano model." *Wikipedia.* https://en.wikipedia.org/wiki/Kano_model

[32] Bonchek, Mark; Bapat, Vivek. "The Most Successful Brands Focus on Users – Not Buyers." *Harvard Business Review.* 7 February 2018. https://hbr.org/2018/02/the-most-successful-brands-focus-on-users-not-buyers

[33] Beaujean, Marc; Davidson, Jonathan; Madge, Stacey. "The 'moment of truth' in customer service." *McKinsey Quarterly.* February 2006. https://www.mckinsey.com/business-functions/organization/our-insights/the-moment-of-truth-in-customer-service

[34] Sinek, Simon. "How great leaders inspire action." *TEDx* Puget Sound. https://www.ted.com/talks/simon_sinek_how_great_leaders_inspire_action/up-next?language=en

[35] Fuke, Roberta. "With great power comes great responsibility: choose your B2B micro-influencer wisely." *B2B Marketing*. 14 January 2019. https://www.b2bmarketing.net/en-gb/resources/blog/great-power-comes-great-responsibility-choose-your-b2b-micro-influencer-wisely

[36] Mehta, Nick. "The Essential Guide to Customer Success." *Gainsight*. https://www.gainsight.com/guides/the-essential-guide-to-customer-success/

[37] Murphy, Lincoln. "Customer success-driven growth." *SixteenVentures*. https://sixteenventures.com

[38] Atkins, Charles; Gupta, Shobhit; Roche, Paul. "Introducing customer success 2.0: The new growth engine." *McKinsey & Company*. January 2018. https://www.mckinsey.com/industries/high-tech/our-insights/introducing-customer-success-2-0-the-new-growth-engine

[39] Mulqueen, Tina. "How To Make The Most Of Customer Insights." *Forbes*. 17 January 2018. https://www.forbes.com/sites/tinamulqueen/2018/01/17/how-to-make-the-most-of-customer-insights/#34bd059321f8

[40] Edelman, David; Heller, Jason. "How digital marketing operations can transform business." *McKinsey & Company*. July 2015. https://www.mckinsey.com/business-functions/marketing-and-sales/our-insights/how-digital-marketing-operations-can-transform-business

Chapter 8

[1] Morris, Dr. Henry. "Improving Business Operation Performance With Innovation." *Digitalist Magazine*. 11 September 2012. https://www.digitalistmag.com/technologies/analytics/2012/09/11/improving-business-operation-performance-with-innovations-09456

[2] "Operations management." *Wikipedia*. https://en.wikipedia.org/wiki/Operations_management

[3] Welch, Chris. "Apple iOS 12: the biggest new features coming to the iPhone." *The Verge*. 12 June 2018. https://www.theverge.com/2018/6/4/17417730/apple-ios-12-iphone-update-best-features-wwdc-2018

[4] "Crude Oil Prices – 70 Year Historical Chart." *Macrotrends*. 2019. https://www.macrotrends.net/1369/crude-oil-price-history-chart

[5] "Retail versus wholesale electricity pricing." *Business Electricity Prices*. https://www.businesselectricityprices.org.uk/retail-versus-wholesale-prices/

[6] "Commodity Prices." *Indexmundi.com*. https://www.indexmundi.com/commodities/

[7] Solon, Olivia. "Facebook faces $1.6bn fine and formal investigation over massive data breach." *The Guardian*. 3 October 2018. https://www.theguardian.com/technology/2018/oct/03/facebook-data-breach-latest-fine-investigation

[8] "British Airways boss apologises for 'malicious' data breach." *BBC News*. 7 September 2018. https://www.bbc.co.uk/news/uk-england-london-45440850

[9] "Walmart Launches Project Gigaton to Reduce Emissions in Company's Supply Chain." *Walmart Press Release*. 19 April 2017. https://news.walmart.com/2017/04/19/walmart-launches-project-gigaton-to-reduce-emissions-in-companys-supply-chain

[10] Whannell, Jeremy. "Giant oil companies go green amid pressure from customers, shareholders." *Born2Invest*. 18 December 2017. https://born2invest.com/articles/giant-oil-companies-go-green-pressure/

[11] "Operational excellence." *Wikipedia*. https://en.wikipedia.org/wiki/Operational_excellence

[12] Okeke, Kelechi. "6 Tech Advances That Will Enhance Customer Experience." *CustomerThink*. 17 September 2018. http://customerthink.com/6-tech-advances-that-will-enhance-customer-experience/

[13] Kerschberg, Ben. "How Digital Disrupts Operations, Business Processes And Customer Experience." *Forbes*. 1 March 2017. https://www.forbes.com/sites/benkerschberg/2017/03/01/how-digital-disrupts-operations-and-business-processes-as-well-as-customer-experience/#bf3f0d354667

[14] Farias, Humberto. "How to incorporate enterprise legacy systems into your digital strategy." *InfoWorld*. 21 March 2018. https://www.infoworld.com/article/3265029/how-to-incorporate-enterprise-legacy-systems-into-your-digital-strategy.html

[15] Krush, Alesia. "12 Kick-Ass Software Prototyping and Mockup Tools." *DZone*. 28 August 2018. https://dzone.com/articles/12-kick-ass-software-prototyping-and-mockup-tools

[16] "Operational responsiveness." *Wikipedia*. https://en.wikipedia.org/wiki/Operational_responsiveness

[17] Kerschberg, Ben. "How Digital Disrupts Operations, Business Processes And Customer Experience." *Forbes*. 1 March 2017. https://www.forbes.com/sites/benkerschberg/2017/03/01/how-digital-disrupts-operations-and-business-processes-as-well-as-customer-experience/#bf3f0d354667

Chapter 9

[1] Pettinger, Tejvan. "Human Capital definition and importance." *Economicshelp*. 22 September 2017. https://www.economicshelp.org/blog/26076/economics/human-capital-definition-and-importance/

[2] Benson-Armer, Richard; Gast, Arne; van Dam, Nick. "Learning at the speed of business." *McKinsey Quarterly*. May 2016. https://www.mckinsey.com/business-functions/organization/our-insights/learning-at-the-speed-of-business

[3] Garton, Eric; Mankins, Michael. "Engaging Your Employees Is Good but Don't Stop There." *Harvard Business Review*. 9 December 2015. https://hbr.org/2015/12/engaging-your-employees-is-good-but-dont-stop-there

[4] Glass, Andy. "People buy from people (is a sales myth)." *Silver Monkey*. 11 March 2014. https://www.silver-monkey.co.uk/people-buy-from-people/

[5] Pelster, Bill; Johnson, Dani; Stempel, Jen; van der Vyver, Bernard. "Careers and learning: Real time, all the time." *Deloitte Insights*. 28 February 2017. https://www2.deloitte.com/insights/us/en/focus/human-capital-trends/2017/learning-in-the-digital-age.html

[6] "The next era of human/machine partnerships." *Institute for the Future & Dell Technologies*. 2017. https://www.delltechnologies.com/content/dam/delltechnologies/assets/perspectives/2030/pdf/SR1940_IFTFforDellTechnologies_Human-Machine_070517_readerhigh-res.pdf

[7] Chadwick, Peter. "What Do CEOs Want from HR? – A White Paper from Henley Business School." *IEDP*. 6 January 2016. https://www.iedp.com/articles/what-do-ceos-want-from-hr/

[8] Bafaro, Frank; Ellsworth, Diana; Gandhi, Neel. "The CEO's guide to competing through HR." *McKinsey Quarterly*. July 2017. https://www.mckinsey.com/business-functions/organization/our-insights/the-ceos-guide-to-competing-through-hr

[9] Agarwal, Dimple; Bersin, Josh; Lahiri, Gaurav; Schwartz, Jeff; Volini, Erica. "The rise of the social enterprise. 2018 Deloitte Global Human Capital Trends." Deloitte Insight. 2018. https://www2.deloitte.com/content/dam/insights/us/articles/HCTrends2018/2018-HCtrends_Rise-of-the-social-enterprise.pdf

[10] Pelster, Bill; Johnson, Dani; Stempel, Jen; van der Vyver, Bernard. "Careers and learning: Real time, all the time." *Deloitte Insights*. 28 February 2017. https://www2.deloitte.com/insights/us/en/focus/human-capital-trends/2017/learning-in-the-digital-age.html

[11] Furniss, Jane; Grounds, David; Sasto, Nathan; Spelman, Mark. "Workforce Planning in the Digital Age." CriticalEye. https://www.criticaleye.com/archive.cfm?id=821

[12] Ogg, Sandy; Kirkland, Rik. "Using talent management to create value." *McKinsey & Company*. January 2017. https://www.mckinsey.com/featured-insights/leadership/using-talent-management-to-create-value

[13] Swords, Professor Dominic. "How HR can be commercial." *Henley Business School, University of Reading*. https://s3-eu-west-1.amazonaws.com/assets.henley.ac.uk/legacyUploads/pdf/exec-ed/How_can_hr_be_commerical.pdf

[14] Kopoulos, Ari. "How to simplify HR processes." *EmployeeConnect*. https://www.employeeconnect.com/blog/how-to-simplify-hr-processes/

[15] Erts, Norberts. "Blockchain in HR: 8 Ways Blockchain will impact the HR Function." *Cake*. 28 October 2018. https://blog.cake.hr/blockchain-in-hr-8-ways-blockchain-will-impact-the-hr-function/

[16] Abbatiello, Anthony; Agarwal, Dimple; Bersin, Josh; Lahiri, Gaurav; Schwartz, Jeff; Volini, Erica. "The rise of the social enterprise. 2018 Deloitte Global Human Capital Trends." *Deloitte Insight*. 2018. https://www2.deloitte.com/content/dam/Deloitte/at/Documents/human-capital/at-2018-deloitte-human-capital-trends.pdf

[17] Gale, Sarah Fister. "Blockchain. The Future of HR?" *Workforce*. 21 May 2018. https://www.workforce.com/2018/05/21/blockchain-future-hr/

[18] Spoke. https://www.askspoke.com

[19] Westfall, Brian. "Robot Resources: What Automation Means for the Future of HR." *Software Advice*. https://www.softwareadvice.com/resources/hr-automation/

[20] Ryan, Brittany. "9 Real-World Examples of Automation in the Workplace." *Spoke*. https://www.askspoke.com/blog/support/examples-automation-workplace/

[21] Yongue, Olivia. "The Impact of Artificial Intelligence in Talent Acquisition." *KRT Marketing*. 23 May 2018. https://www.krtmarketing.com/blog/artificial-intelligence-talent-acquisition/

[22] "Innovation of the Day: Spot" *TrendWatching*. 12 December 2018. http://info.trendwatching.com/bot-takes-the-human-out-of-human-resources?utm_campaign=Innovation%20of%20the%20Day%20&utm_source=hs_email&utm_medium=email&utm_content=68236366&_hsenc=p2ANqtz-8t5BFGxP3BNOYkGY7U2y8m-ySIM3tDCgh8P46zWZwV8cjPPGI_TPghWzSjkJdcYOqwKW8L1Ay9LqgPjuihgtK503IABQ&_hsmi=68236845

[23] Pelster, Bill; Johnson, Dani; Stempel, Jen; van der Vyver, Bernard. "Careers and learning: Real time, all the time." *Deloitte Insights*. 28 February 2017. https://www2.deloitte.com/insights/us/en/focus/human-capital-trends/2017/learning-in-the-digital-age.html

[24] *Grohappy*. https://www.grohappy.co.uk

[25] Abbatiello, Anthony; Agarwal, Dimple; Bersin, Josh; Lahiri, Gaurav; Schwartz, Jeff; Volini, Erica. "The rise of the social enterprise. 2018 Deloitte Global Human Capital Trends." *Deloitte Insight*. 2018. https://www2.deloitte.com/content/dam/Deloitte/at/Documents/human-capital/at-2018-deloitte-human-capital-trends.pdf

45904375R00110

Printed in Poland
by Amazon Fulfillment
Poland Sp. z o.o., Wrocław